D1605842

YEAR-ROUND SCHOOLING

YEAR-ROUND SCHOOLING

Promises and Pitfalls

**Carolyn M. Shields and
Steven Lynn Oberg**

The Scarecrow Press, Inc.
Technomic Books
Lanham, Maryland, and London
2000

SCARECROW PRESS, INC.
Technomic Books

Published in the United States of America
by Scarecrow Press, Inc.
4720 Boston Way, Lanham, Maryland 20706
http://www.scarecrowpress.com

4 Pleydell Gardens, Folkestone
Kent CT20 2DN, England

British Library Cataloguing in Publication Information Available

Library of Congress Cataloging-in-Publication Data

Shields, Carolyn M.
    Year-round schooling : promises and pitfalls / Carolyn M. Shields and
Steven Lynn Oberg.
    p. cm.
"Technomic Books."
Includes bibliographical references and index.
ISBN 0-8108-3744-7 (cloth : alk. paper)
    1. Year-round schools—United States.   2. School management and
organization—United States.   I. Oberg, Steven Lynn.   II. Title.

LB3034 .S55   2000
371.2'36'0973—dc21   00-020501

CONTENTS

FIGURES

ACRONYMS

CAVE	Citizens Against Virtually Everything
ESL	English as a second language
GED	Graduation equivalency diploma
LAUSD	Los Angeles Unified School District
LEP	Limited English proficiency
LYNT	Last year's new thing
MT-YRS	Multi-track year-round school
MT	Multi-track
PAM	Parents Against Multi-tracking
SAT	Stanford Achievement Test
SES	Socioeconomic status
ST	Single-track
ST-YRS	Single-track year-round school
TCS	Traditional calendar school
TYC	Traditional year calendar
TYNT	This year's new thing
YR	Year-round
YRE	Year-round education
YRS	Year-round school or year-round schooling

ACKNOWLEDGMENTS

We would like to thank all of the students, parents, and educators with whom we have had the opportunity of working as we compiled information for this book. We were privileged to meet a large number of district administrators, school principals, and teachers who were dedicated to excellence in their fields and who dispelled the popular myth that educators are resistant to change. Many of the superintendents from some of the largest and most complex districts in North America took time to personally escort us around their districts, to show us their facilities, and to introduce us to school personnel. We are grateful for their interest, insights, facilitation of our site-based data collection, and for their generosity in sharing district data, documents, and test scores with us.

Classroom teachers, increasingly challenged by their changing roles and by pressures to enact new initiatives, generously gave their time to talk to us at length regarding the impact of various school-year calendars and to distribute and administer student and parent surveys. Without them, this book could not have been written.

We thank the parents and students who completed our surveys for their insights, opinions, and perspectives. Many took time to write extensive comments and to reflect carefully on related educational and community issues. Others spent time informally discussing the issues raised and sharing their perspectives on YRS.

Many other people also contributed to the research behind this book. The National Association of Year-Round Education (NAYRE) helped us significantly by providing unpublished documents from their collection and by making available up-to-date data concerning the prevalence of year-round school calendars. Individual researchers and representatives of teacher unions and parent councils have increased our understanding of the complexity of school calendar change, both by agreeing with and by challenging our interpretations and perspectives. Their insights have helped us to better reflect on why some initiatives seem so successful, while others, similar in appearance and structure, attract so much controversy and dissatisfaction.

Finally, we acknowledge the Social Sciences and Humanities Research Council of Canada (SSHRC), without whose funding of this major longitudinal and international project, we could never have accomplished this research. Without the ability to travel extensively and to examine many of the variations of alternate school year calendars across North America, neither this book nor our other publications on YRS could have been written. The comprehensive nature of this research and the extensive contacts we have made with policy makers and practitioners have allowed this project to have a significant impact on educational policy, the implementation of modified calendars, and on the practice of year-round education in districts across the United States and Canada.

Despite heated debate over the substantial as well as the trivial aspects of the book, we are still speaking to each other. The lengthy, often difficult and challenging process has been a time of learning—about year-round education and about collaboration. It has been a pleasure writing this book on YRS. We hope it will assist you in your reflections on, and discussions about, changes in school year calendars as well as other substantive educational reforms.

INTRODUCTION

A school board member from New Mexico is convinced that year-round school is one of "a lot of gimmicks in education that are re-introduced every twenty or twenty-five years." He likens the process to "infatuation with change for change's sake" or "re-invention of the flat tire." (Worsnop, 1996, p. 438)

*****

Educational policy makers could simply choose to live with the diminished learning opportunities and decay in skills that accompany the present dominant school calendar. However, [I] suggest that policy makers who take this position . . . must also state why an optimal pedagogical strategy ought not include both an alternative calendar and more efficient use of time. (Cooper et al., 1996, p. 263)

*****

One superintendent reported receiving two telephone calls from parents. One asked, "Once my child is on a year-round schedule, will I at least see him on weekends?" The other wondered, "After the school adopts a year-round schedule, will my child be able to spend Christmas Day with our family?"

*****

Year-round schooling (YRS) is a term that gives rise to very strong opinions and often to considerable confusion. The term *year-round schooling* is actually a misnomer that seems to suggest that students are in school all year long. In fact, there are many different models and configurations of year-round schooling, most of which have the same number of days as the traditional school year. What is

I

common to all of them is that the year-round schedule takes the long summer vacation of the traditional calendar and redistributes it more evenly throughout the year, allowing for year-round use of facilities.

Our goal in writing this book is to provide a balanced look at year-round schooling, examine some of the various models commonly in use, present some illustrations from practical experience, summarize the current research, and reflect on some contextual issues related to implementation. This book will help the reader to better understand the impact, drawbacks, and potential of year-round schooling as a possible educational alternative for the next century.

HISTORICAL OVERVIEW OF SCHOOL CALENDARS

The dominant North American school calendar, typically referred to as *traditional*, has been in effect for more than a century. By the middle of the 19th century, several different calendars had been developed. In rural areas, the school year originally lasted for five to six months (often from the last harvest to the first planting), whereas in many urban areas, schools were open almost year-round (usually for 11 or 12 months). In 1847, curricular modifications to address the newly implemented grade-level organization of schools were beginning to be introduced (Glines, 1988). These, in turn, led to a gradual move to a more uniform calendar. To offer a standard curriculum, urban schools reduced the length of their year and rural areas increased the number of school days to what we have come to know as the agrarian calendar, a year with approximately nine months of schooling and a three-month summer break. By 1894, the shorter urban school year had brought a number of critiques, including one from the U.S. Commissioner of Education, William T. Harris, who lamented the reduced number of school days in this way: "The boy of today must attend school 11.1 years in order to receive as much instruction, quantitatively, as the boy of 50 years ago received in eight years" (National Education Commission, 1994, p. 31).

In the early 1900s, a small number of urban areas re-established year-round schedules to meet the changing needs of their populations. During that time, what some regard as the first modern year-round schools were instituted in Bluffton, Ohio, in 1904, Newark,

New Jersey, in 1912, and Minot, North Dakota, in 1917. Glines (1988) indicates that

> They were begun for many reasons. Newark did it to help immigrants learn English and to enable students to accelerate; Bluffton did it to improve curriculum and learning and to provide family and student options . . . and Minot did it to meet the needs of the "laggards." (p. 17)

Brinkerhoff, an educational researcher of the 1930s, reported the success of these schools. He stated that what were then called *all-year schools* graduated "a higher percentage of their pupils; they show a lower grade age; they have less retardation; they lose fewer pupils before graduating." Moreover, Brinkerhoff saw no evidence of "brain fatigue, loss of mental health, or impaired physical development" (cited in Doyle & Finn, 1985, p. 31). New economic and social pressures prevented these early forms of year-round schooling from persisting beyond the Depression and World War II.

In 1969, the concept of year-round schooling was simultaneously revived in communities in four states: California, Illinois, Minnesota, and Missouri (Glines, 1988, p. 17). This resurgence was specifically intended to address rapid population growth and overcrowding of schools. Within the next decade, a number of other communities and districts opted for year-round schooling because of its potential to enhance learning. More recently, a combination of factors has contributed to the increasingly large numbers of students in year-round schools: changing immigration and migration patterns, political and fiscal pressures, higher expectations regarding school completion, and tighter job markets. Modern schools are also assailed by the need to institute special programs, for instance, limited English proficiency (LEP), academically talented and gifted classes, English as a second language instruction (ESL), special education, and vocational training. By 1999, according to statistics published by the National Association of Year-Round Education, there were more than two million students in 2931 year-round schools located in 597 districts in the United States alone.

OVERVIEW OF YEAR-ROUND SCHOOLING

Despite the growing presence of YRS, there is no single generally accepted model that has been adopted in all districts. This has led to confusion and misunderstanding about the innovation. Although some districts use the terms *all-year schools* and *year-round schools* to represent an 11 month calendar, year-round schooling is most often used to describe the calendar modification that requires students to begin school earlier and end later than normal. But rather than extend the school year, most districts then redistribute the "lost" summer time in vacation blocks throughout the year. Some districts add a few minutes to the length of individual school days and reduce the total number of days in the academic year, permitting their schools to better accommodate overlapping schedules. Still others offer the possibility of extending the school year by offering classes during school vacations (intersession) on a voluntary basis.

There are, however, two main forms of year-round schooling, each introduced for specific reasons. A single-track (ST) calendar is usually implemented to provide a more balanced and enriched educational program or to accommodate the special scheduling needs of a unique community. Schools on this schedule often begin the academic year early in August, with students and teachers on a cycle of 45 days in school, followed by 15 days of vacation time. During this three-week period, known as intersession, schools frequently offer remedial, enrichment, or special-interest programs for students and sometimes parents. This schedule has helped to address family needs in some communities where one or two major industries or employers demand that the parents work unusual schedules. For instance, in resort communities, where summer is a required work period and vacations may best be taken in the spring or fall, an alternate schedule may be beneficial.

The multi-track (MT) calendar is usually enacted in an attempt to keep up with rapidly increasing enrollment or when the pressures of government cost-cutting force districts to look for ways to house a growing number of students in existing facilities. Because the organization of students in classes is staggered with some being on vacation while others are in class, MT-YRS permits districts to accommodate more children in existing buildings. For example, a school that could normally house 600 students on a traditional or single-track schedule could serve 800 on a four-track schedule by rotating groups of 200 students and their teachers throughout the year.

Despite the growing number of year-round schools, the traditional calendar is still very much the norm across the United States and Canada where the force of more than a century of tradition makes changing the calendar extremely difficult. These challenges are, of course, not unexpected of an innovation that appears to threaten the thinking and social practice of 100 years of North American society.

As with any innovation, year-round schooling is not without both proponents and detractors. This frequently gives rise to lively debate and to a number of controversies. Some proponents claim that YRS will be a panacea for society's ills, save billions of dollars, and generally result in better education for all students. They also promise that YRS will result in a reduction of vandalism and crime, fewer school dropouts, the elimination of portable classrooms, a decrease in capital cost outlays, less forgetting, a shorter time needed for review of academic material, and a general increase in student performance. Some opponents, on the other hand, are concerned about the impact of YRS on the school, the family, the community, and even on the moral fabric of society itself. They claim that it will destroy school unity, increase teacher workload, make deep cleaning of school facilities impossible, eliminate the possibility of family vacations, disrupt community recreational activities, and in general, erode traditional family values.

The academic literature is equally divided, with a large number of articles written to support either an advocacy or oppositional position. Many studies have been commissioned to determine the early success or failure of year-round education in specific districts. There has been little data-based research of a longitudinal nature and much of the empirical work to date has consisted of surveys of pre-implementation concerns. Many newspaper and magazine articles have perpetuated some of the concerns and misunderstandings about year-round schooling or have exaggerated its benefits for a specific school or district. Some articles are based on solid research. Overall, however, the body of writing about YRS contains numerous generalizations and oversimplifications of what is really a very complex issue.

OVERVIEW OF THE BOOK

Until now, there have been no comprehensive books on year-round schooling. We hope this book will fill the gap. It is not a "how-to" book in the tradition of those that provide worksheets, checklists, and an implementation guide. Instead, we see the value of this book primarily in terms of helping people to understand and reflect on the issues related to a calendar change. For those who want information about other resources or our ongoing research projects, see Appendix B.

The book is laid out in the following manner. In the first section, *Models and Practice*, we present an overview of some of the commonly used models of year-round schooling. In each of the three chapters, we describe some specific calendars and share stories of several schools that have implemented them. The first chapter focuses on single-track year-round schooling, community-based approaches, and dual-track calendar modifications. Chapter 2 examines multi-track scheduling with its overlapping and rotating structures. While the first two chapters deal with year-round schooling primarily as an elementary school phenomenon, Chapter 3 outlines its implementation, in both single and multi-track forms, as employed in secondary schools.

The second section, *Research and Perspectives*, presents a data based examination of the impact of year-round schooling and of the attitudes of various groups. Chapter 4 examines the relationship between YRS and academic and non-academic student outcomes. In Chapters 5, 6, and 7, we draw from our research to describe, in turn, the perceptions and experiences of parents, teachers, and administrators with year-round schooling.

In the third section, *The Broader Context,* we introduce a variety of topics to provoke reflection and discussion. Many of these are issues that need to be considered but appear to have been frequently overlooked or discounted by those investigating year-round schooling. They include questions of support, commitment, equity, and voice. In Chapter 8, we examine the social and cultural context of schools in communities. Chapter 9 raises concerns related to democratic processes and the politicization of education. In Chapter 10, the focus is on fiscal considerations related to the costs and benefits of year-round schooling.

In the conclusion, we present a framework for a comprehensive examination of any educational reform initiative. The matrix will help explain the complex issues related to the successful implementation of YRS. We conclude by exploring the relationship of a new calendar to wider issues of assessment, leadership, and educational change.

Throughout the book, we use pseudonyms for the individuals, schools, and districts that have generously and openly participated in our research projects. This is intended to protect their anonymity and prevent any errors, which are entirely ours, from reflecting on them. It is also in recognition that schools are fluid organizations and that, although our descriptions are accurate for a specific point in time, changes in structure, leadership, and even philosophy may have occurred since our last visits. Thus, our use of pseudonyms emphasizes the element of possibility that is inherent in this discussion of YRS. We refer to specific schools and individuals, not so much for what they have done or said, but as illustrations of ways in which others have thought about school year calendar changes. However, where proper names are an intrinsic part of a historical overview or appear in published reports, we use them as published.

The figures in this book are taken from actual calendars used by some of the schools we visited. They are only examples of the hundreds of different possible permutations. Please note that they may not agree exactly with our text.

We hope this book will be useful to anyone who wants to better understand the myths and potentials, the promises and pitfalls, of year-round schooling. It is also our hope that it will initiate lively conversation and constructive debate that will lead to creative solutions for improving the educational experiences of both educators and students.

SECTION I:

MODELS AND PRACTICE

In this section, we describe several different models of year-round schooling, known in some jurisdictions as alternative or modified calendars. Although there are almost as many calendars as there are school districts involved in year-round schooling, we highlight a few common approaches used in elementary schools as well as some of the variations used in secondary schools.

In Chapter 1, we discuss some elementary-school models of single-track year-round schooling, including what we are calling community-based models and a relatively unique dual-track schedule that combines modified and traditional calendars within the same school. Chapter 2 presents several different modifications of multi-track year-round schooling at the elementary level. The third chapter focuses on how secondary schools may implement both single- and multi-track approaches.

The models presented and the schools described exist, of course, within specific political, educational, and legal contexts that help to shape the innovation in particular ways. A more complete discussion of some of these contextual factors, including some differing motivations for instituting year-round schooling, the cultural, fiscal, and political climates within which it occurs, and the impact of community control and empowerment on the innovation, occurs in Section III.

To accompany the examination of each type of calendar, we also present a summary and discussion of some of the current literature. As we note in each chapter, the quality and utility of the literature varies, regardless of the quantity that might be available. For example, in some instances, reports and reviews focus on perceptions and opinions of people who have had no first-hand knowledge of (and, consequently, may have developed many misconceptions about) year-round schooling. In some cases, articles report experiences that took place more than a quarter century ago, when the educational contexts and philosophies were quite different from those of today.

In each of the next three chapters, we provide an overview of the unique characteristics of some models of YR calendars and of some current research. We use vignettes of schools that have implemented various approaches to give a sense of what each model looks like in practice and to lay the groundwork for the section that summarizes what are generally considered to be the major disadvantages or benefits of the calendar under examination.

CHAPTER 1:

SINGLE-TRACK AND COMMUNITY-BASED
YEAR-ROUND SCHOOLING

By modifying the school calendar a little, offering choice, and inviting parents to be involved in an intersession activity with their children, we had the director of the community center shaking his head. He couldn't imagine, in his lifetime, getting those 70 parents involved in their children's schooling. All we did was give them the opportunity; we didn't beat the bushes, knock on doors, advertise extensively, or anything. Ten percent more parent involvement in just one week! (Elementary school principal)

*****

The most prevalent form of year-round schooling, single-track (ST-YRS), is introduced almost exclusively for educational reasons. In 1999, of all schools in the United States and Canada reporting some type of year-round calendar, approximately 60% had instituted some form of single-track schedule. In this ST-YR schedule, the school calendar is altered to permit a shorter summer vacation and an allocation of vacation periods in a more balanced way throughout the school year. In general, although students spend the same amount of time in school as their peers on traditional schedules, the school year begins earlier, ends later, and redistributes students' in-class and vacation times. Often, during their vacation period, generally called intersession, students have the opportunity to participate in a variety of educational activities for remediation or enrichment. The appellation *single-track*, which applies to the whole school, is used to distinguish this schedule from the sometimes more controversial multi-track schedule that involves groups of students rotating on different schedules called *tracks*.

Although there are several reasons generally given for the adoption of a single-track schedule, most focus on providing better learning opportunities for students, a less stressful schedule for teachers, and a more balanced school year for families at little additional cost to the school district. The following comments are typical of the responses to single-track year-round schooling found in our parent surveys and teacher interviews.

- It just makes sense.
- It is a better way to educate kids.
- The agrarian calendar is antiquated.
- Kids retain more. They forget less.
- Kids get so bored over the long summer. They are ready to come back to school. . . .

You will note that all of the above responses were favorable to single-track year-round calendars. In our research, the responses were overwhelmingly positive. The few negative comments we received related to the adaptation of family schedules, particularly arranging for childcare and coordinating family vacations when other siblings attended schools on different schedules.

In this chapter, we describe some single-track, community-based, and dual-track schedules, explore the concept of intersession, and present some illustrations of their implementation. We also provide an overview of the relevant literature, describe the use of single-track models as a means of transition to multi-track schedules, and summarize some disadvantages and benefits of ST-YRS.

SOME FREQUENTLY USED SINGLE-TRACK MODELS

In a very common variation of single-track year-round schooling (ST-YRS), known as the 45-15 model, students attend school for 45 days followed by a 15-day vacation break. The sequence is repeated four times to complete the academic year about the end of June. This model is shown in Figure 1.1. Note that in this illustration, school begins in July and follows a regular pattern of schooling and breaks, with students and teachers benefiting from all of the traditional holidays as well as enjoying their vacation time throughout the year. In addition, teachers have the opportunity to participate

Figure 1.1 Single-track 180 day calendar.

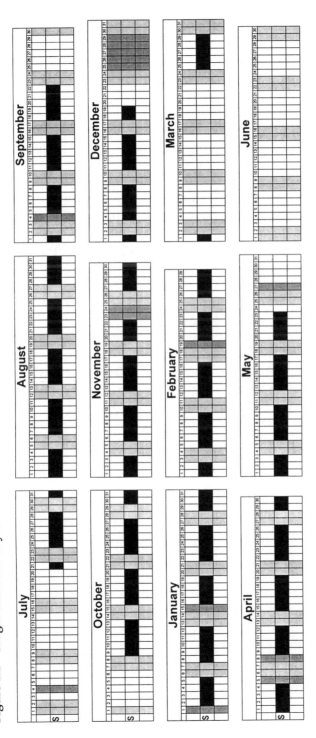

S = Single-track

in district-designated days for professional development activities as well as teachers' association conferences.

In another common variation of the ST calendar, some schools have adopted a schedule consisting of three sessions of 60 days in school with subsequent vacation periods of 20 days. Not all districts, however, facilitate such equal distribution of in-class and vacation periods. Some have adopted quite irregular calendars that, they feel, still offer most of the benefits of a single-track calendar.[1] One less regular calendar is presented in Figure 1.2. It comes from a district with high summer mobility in which there was a perception that many people moved into the area over the summer and were unable to take full advantage of a schedule that began in August. In some instances, students arrived at the school, ready to register, after school had been in session for a month. In this case, the district decided that a move away from an August start would also maintain funding based on the greatest possible enrollment.

In another model, although students do not attend the whole time, school is in session for 220 days during the year. The students are shown a school-year calendar and given the option of choosing the 180 days during which they will be present in school. This flexibility requires considerable individualization of instruction and extended teacher contracts but, by allowing individual choice, seems also to result in maximum student attendance.

Intersession Programs

Many schools choose to offer what are commonly known as intersession programs during the breaks between regular school sessions. Again, there are innumerable options with intersession activities taking various forms. In some districts that offer summer school funding, schools have been able to reallocate these monies and to provide special programs for kids. In other districts, special grants have been procured to fund intersession. Elsewhere, where there are no funds for additional programs, schools have offered intersession on a cost-recovery basis—frequently at a lower cost to parents than daycare. Some schools have asked for an activity fee for participating students but have invited parents to accompany

[1]For some other calendar variations, see Appendix A.

Figure 1.2 Irregular single-track calendar.

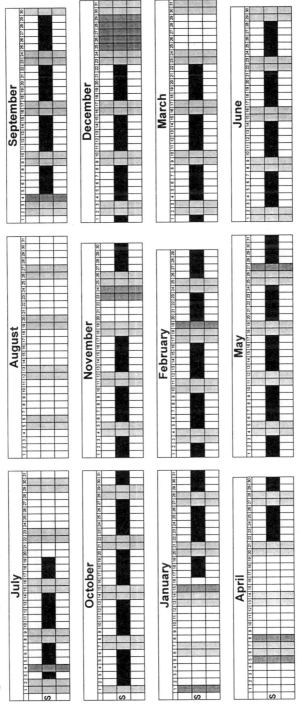

S = Single-track

their children free of charge. This option has had the effect of garnering parental involvement in, and support for, the school as well
as providing additional adult supervision for students. Still other
schools have invited local groups such as Parks and Recreation or
the YWCA to offer recreational activities, sports, swimming lessons,
or crafts during school breaks.

One example of an innovative program is provided by Warrick-
Harris (1995). In an effort to meet the needs of its rapidly growing
population, an elementary school in North Carolina implemented
some calendar changes that included a creative approach to intersession. For the first off-track week, low-cost childcare was provided from 6:30 AM to 6:00 PM. During the second week, enrichment
activities were offered through field trips, crafts, and projects in the
morning with optional afternoon childcare for those who needed
it. This program was offered at a fee of $25 for five mornings. In
the third week, students identified as needing academic assistance
received a half-day remedial program, supported by free bus transportation. This portion of the intersession was financed by a redistribution of summer school funds. For all three weeks, lunch was
available as usual at the regular price.

Although some schools offer the intersession programs as
activity-oriented enrichment type activities, others concentrate primarily on academic offerings ranging from targeted remedial programs to enrichment activities for gifted and talented students.
Some, as the North Carolina school described above, have opted for
a combination. The range of opportunities is limited only by the initiative and creativity of those in charge. The following vignette provides one example of innovative approaches to ST-YRS.

Provost Elementary School[2]

In Provost Elementary School, the teachers described their fight for
permission to implement a single-track schedule. They had held
parent meetings, conducted surveys, and stormed the local board
office with demands to change to the single-track schedule, one that
they perceived would enable them to better meet the needs of their
student body. The teachers were convinced that many students

[2]All names of schools and individuals from our research are pseudonyms.

would benefit from the additional weeks of remediation or enrichment offered by intersession. They hoped that the year-round schedule would prevent children from being "street kids" during the long summer months, would provide a secure place for students to congregate, and would hook them into learning by providing more interactive, integrated learning opportunities in a relaxed environment where testing was not seen as threatening.

Intersession in Provost School was offered for a period of two weeks (of the three-week break) between each of the regular nine-week terms at a cost of $44 to parents and further subsidized by funds from grants and outside sources. The intention of intersession was to utilize creative approaches to instruction with the aim of increasing the motivation and enthusiasm of students for learning. One of the teachers spoke of how every student has gifts. She stated that the staff shared a belief that, although the regular approach to schooling did not permit each gift to be identified and to flourish, the intersession structure might. Examples of creative approaches to teaching were abundant. One teacher taught geometry through string art where students learned to use protractors and rulers to create the intricate patterns. Another used the creation of a school version of a "Little Rascals" video to teach communication skills. A third used papier maché to create models to help teach about nature and the environment. We were told that at the end of each intersession period, a public celebration of learning included displays and student performances. Teachers reported that students expressed delight in the high quality of their achievements and demonstrated increased motivation for learning.

This was exactly what the teachers had hoped would happen when they moved to the single-track schedule. However, we were also told that despite the generally positive experience, there had been some disappointments. Unpredictable and decreasing funding available for the intersession program had shifted the teaching responsibilities from certified teachers to non-certified teacher aides. This had tended to routinize the offerings and reduce teacher enthusiasm about the program. In turn, this was reported to have led to less teacher interaction about innovative approaches to teaching and learning than expected and to have reduced the potential impact on their regular classroom practice.

Teachers in Provost School also expressed the concern that not all of the students who could benefit from the intersession programs actually attended them. They were discouraged that some parents did not seem to understand the educational benefits of intersession: some acceded to their children's requests for unencumbered vacation time. Some teachers thought that other parents sent their children because it offered a cheaper and better solution to childcare than conventional babysitting services. Despite these concerns, the intersession program continued to be popular. During the school's first four years on the single-track calendar, intersession regularly attracted more than 50% of the student body.

In addition to the implementation of intersession, teachers in Provost School sought other ways to address the learning needs of their students. Two years after the school moved to a single-track schedule, two other innovations were implemented on a pilot basis: two multi-age cross-grade classes and a critical thinking program were introduced. By the next year, the innovations had become so popular with both teachers and parents that it was difficult both to maintain the traditional grade-level classes and to fulfill parental requests for placement in multi-age cross-grade groupings.

Each of these innovations—intersession, new teaching strategies, critical thinking, and multi-age cross-grade groupings—facilitated more thematic and holistic approaches to instruction and offered teachers increased opportunities to address the learning needs and styles of their students. In some instances, this was expedited through closer relationships developed during the smaller intersession classes and, in others, through the opportunity to have the same students in a multi-age grouping for more than one year.

Teachers in Provost School linked the need for innovation to their personal philosophies that each child could learn. They believed that, for their under-achieving students, it might take more effort and innovation on the part of the teacher to find appropriate learning strategies and to create supportive learning environments, but that their efforts would pay off. They repeatedly stated that the move to a single-track calendar had facilitated both intersession activities and the other innovations that they had instituted. They believed that the multi-age cross-grade groupings could not have happened at their school without the change of calendar.

This snapshot of Provost Elementary School is just one of many that could be shared to give some of the flavor of a single-track year-round school and how it might be organized to provide additional learning opportunities for children. The experience of this school is important because it demonstrates that a YR calendar may provide the impetus for a series of additional changes designed to improve a school's educational program.

COMMUNITY-BASED OPTIONS

In most areas, schools and districts have implemented one of the calendars described above; however, in a number of communities, other responsive approaches have been used. Some of the most interesting modifications of the single-track schedule are in Canada, where year-round schooling is still relatively new. In what we are calling a *community-based approach*, some educators who wanted to change their calendars began by inviting parents and other community members to provide feedback about the desirability of modifications to the school calendar.

In a logging community in northern British Columbia, a small school, faced with declining enrollment and the possibility of imminent closure, decided to implement a year-round calendar designed to meet the needs of that specific community. Although loggers are able to work during the winter and summer months, during both the spring thaw and fall freeze-up periods, roads into the forests are impassable. In developing an alternative calendar, the school council took this community employment downtime into consideration and scheduled three-week vacations during each of these periods. In this case, the innovative calendar was so effective that the school began to draw students from logging families throughout the district, an arrangement the district supported by providing bussing.

In another instance, a private, band-administered, First Nations[3] school operated a single-track calendar that began in August and provided vacation time to coincide with the beginning of the hunting and fishing seasons. They also organized the schedule and curriculum around their particular traditional activities. For example, during fishing season they developed units relating to local activities, such as net mending and understanding the salmon run,

[3]The term *First Nations* is used frequently in Canada, particularly in the West, to refer to aboriginal (Indian) populations. Indian bands (tribes) sometimes operate their own schools; sometimes, they contract with a neighboring school district to provide educational services for their students.

through which they fulfilled the prescribed provincial learning objectives. For them, the calendar change facilitated curricular adaptation that more closely met the needs of their specific community.

In the Northwest Territories, the Ministry of Education introduced legislation that permits schools and districts to modify the school calendar within certain parameters. There, many Innuit[4] schools also adapt their calendar to accommodate their particular fishing and hunting seasons. In these communities, the year-round schedule has proven to be not only a viable, but also a desirable, alternative to the traditional calendar.

A Combined Calendar: Providing an Option

In some of the community-based options we studied, we found that implementation had been gradual, with some parents and students in a school opting for a modified calendar that began three or four weeks ahead of the traditional school year and others maintaining their traditional schedule. This modification, sometimes called dual-track (or school-within-a-school), offers those who wish to move to a year-round schedule the opportunity to do so, while maintaining some classes in the same school on a traditional schedule for those who prefer not to change.

In one K-8 school, a retired principal was invited into the school to meet with students to receive input related to a calendar change. He presented classes with blank calendars and asked students to indicate when they felt they would be ready to return to school after a summer vacation and when they thought it would be helpful to have additional vacation time during the year. Parents were invited to participate in a similar process. The result was a combined calendar that offered both a traditional schedule and a modified one. The latter began three weeks ahead of the rest of the district and offered, in addition to the other regularly scheduled holidays, one-week breaks in October, March, and May.

In a neighboring school, a similar process brought about a slightly different result. The dual-track approach combined a tra-

[4]*Innuit* is the term commonly used in Canada to refer to indigenous Eskimo populations.

ditional calendar with a concurrent modified calendar that started four weeks in advance, inserting one-week breaks in October, February, March, and May.

The difference between the dual-track model and what we have called single track is that the calendar change is not an "all-or-nothing" occurrence. In most cases, students, parents, and teachers may, if they wish, remain on the traditional schedule, whereas those who wish to experiment with modifications to the school year may do so—all within the same school. Thus, the dual-track calendar offers patrons, teachers, and students increased choice and control over their educational schedule.

In some instances, the dual-track calendar provides an incremental approach to change, permitting gradual implementation of a modified calendar as people become more familiar with it. In the first year-round school in Ontario, implementation was so gradual that the school began with one multi-age, cross-grade class of 30 fourth, fifth, and sixth grade students. In the following four years, the modified calendar increased in popularity and permitted four classes, representing roughly one third of the total school population, (organized in classes of grades 1-3, 4-5, 5-6, 7-8) to be offered. Although there was always a waiting list for the modified calendar classes, the need to maintain balance in class size on both schedules prevented the accommodation of everyone who desired a change.

Figure 1.3 contains an example of a dual-track schedule used in a school with approximately 50% of its students on each calendar. As in some other places, this school also offered a slightly altered schedule prior to Labor Day. The staff opted to run the school day from 8:30 AM to 2:30 PM instead of the 9:00 AM to 3:15 PM time period in force from September to June. Reducing the time allocated to recess and lunch periods permitted students and their families to continue to enjoy summer activities together in August.

Most of the community-based approaches we investigated took advantage of learning opportunities not usually available during the regular school calendar. One chose to offer swimming lessons in an adjacent community outdoor pool at the beginning of the modified school year. (This was unavailable to the traditional calendar because the pool closed at the end of August.) Another school took small groups of its modified calendar students, for a week at a time, for instruction centered in the nearby Pioneer Village. Some teachers developed interdisciplinary and thematic units that could

Figure 1.3 Dual-track calendar

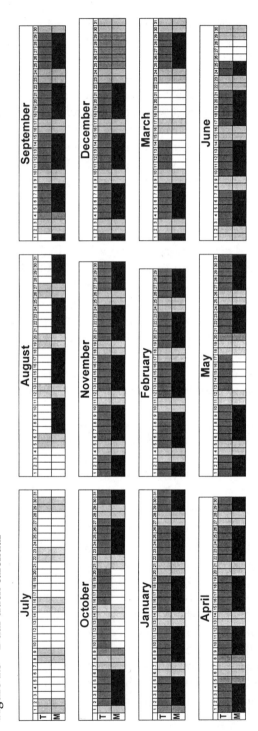

T = Traditional calendar schedule

M = Modified calendar

be operated in such facilities as local museums or provincial and national parks with interpretive centers—many of which also normally closed prior to school opening.

One school, where the modified schedule offered a three-week advance start, had originally been built to facilitate team teaching and open classroom concepts and had many classrooms with sliding walls between them. During the six weeks when students from each schedule were in class while the others were not, the walls were moved back and students benefited from the extra space and from double computer access by using the stations from the partner class as well.

It is possible for dual-track schools to offer intersession programs when some students are off-track. In one school, these weeks were used to link the school and the community. When opportunities were offered to students during the one-week vacation periods to participate in field trips or learning activities held at outside locations (for example, the nearby Science Center), children were required to pay their transportation and admission fees, but parents were allowed to come as supervisors at no charge. This had the unanticipated effect of increasing direct parent involvement in their children's education, providing families with opportunities they otherwise might not have had, and garnering additional support for school activities. (This initiative was particularly beneficial in involving parents from lower socioeconomic groups.) In fact, after the first week in which this was tried, some parents scheduled their own vacations to coincide with the next school break so they could again participate in some low-cost educational and social activities with their children. The school addressed issues of equity by permitting the community-based program to extend into the traditional-calendar classes as well, with classes on the regular schedule allowed to participate as their teachers wished.

SINGLE-TRACK YEAR-ROUND SCHOOLING AS A TRANSITION TO A MULTI-TRACK CALENDAR

One additional aspect of single-track year-round schooling seems worthy of mention at this point. Single-track schedules are sometimes implemented as a means of transition from a traditional calendar to a multi-track year-round schedule.

A large western U.S. district also used a form of single-track schedule as a way of effecting a smooth transition to multi-track year-round schooling in its new buildings. Two new schools, completed in the fall of 1995, opened as single-track schools to permit the staff and students to become well acquainted with each other, to facilitate the development of school policy, and to support the emerging sense of school community. The scheduled move to a multi-track calendar the following year took place without difficulty and without notable opposition by educators or dissent from any of the relatively affluent parent groups represented in the school communities.

In the Pacific Northwest, another school chose to begin on a single-track calendar as an intentional and strategic choice to convince members of the teachers' union (on record as opposing year-round education) that a YR calendar would not be detrimental and would not contravene the provisions or principles of their contract. Although it was not thought that enrollment growth would be as rapid as it actually was, the school opened as a single-track school in anticipation of a move to a multi-track calendar as enrollment required. Their initial success and continued enthusiasm for the new calendar led to the adoption of a policy to facilitate the subsequent move to a multi-track schedule. This was a move that could never have happened in that district without the prior successful experience with ST-YRS.

A dual-track calendar can also facilitate a change to a more extensive multi-track schedule. One dual-track school requested that its board permit the implementation of a magnet school for an arts-infused curriculum that would operate on a third, overlapping modified schedule. The principal and faculty dreamed of adding a fourth track to accommodate a magnet program for gifted and talented students.

In each of these examples, a change to a single-track year-round calendar was not the goal but merely the first step in the staff's attempt to reconsider and improve its educational programs. Although a change of calendar is sometimes used to help with a transition that is potentially difficult or disruptive, this is not always the case. In a district in the Midwest, change seems to be a way of life. There, all elementary schools are on some form of year-round calendar and have been for several decades. When the area population increases for a given school, it moves to a MT calendar; when the population declines, a ST schedule is re-introduced.

Overall, single-track year-round schooling seems to serve well a variety of educational and organizational purposes.

WHAT DOES THE LITERATURE SAY ABOUT SINGLE-TRACK YEAR-ROUND SCHOOLING?

In general, much of the literature on year-round schooling fails to distinguish between studies conducted in single-track schools and those related to the multi-track calendar. In some instances, there is no way to determine which calendar is being studied; in others, it takes a careful reading of the whole article to identify the appropriate schedule. Sometimes, the literature carefully describes accompanying intersession programs; elsewhere, there is no mention of whether additional remediation or enrichment is offered or whether attendance at intersession is voluntary or mandatory. This makes it difficult to determine the effects of a single-track calendar on student academic and non-academic outcomes.

The following overview may, however, be helpful in providing additional information concerning single-track elementary schools. Matheson (1993) states that San Diego decided to offer, in addition to its multi-track elementary schedule, a single-track 45-15 calendar to "create a better learning environment for the students" (p. 35). The Virginia State Department of Education (1992), although not specifically addressing student learning in year-round schools, discusses the relationship between time in school and student learning and recognizes that time alone, without quality instruction, does not necessarily result in improvements in student learning (p. 14). The report suggests that the short-term nature of many studies combined with poor research designs may account for many inconclusive findings related to programs such as intersession. Nevertheless, the authors conclude that the jury is still out on the effects of intersession.

Others (Allinder et al., 1992; Cooper et al., 1996), examining the learning loss of students over the long summer months, found that students who were "disadvantaged" benefit considerably by having a shorter summer break. Greenfield (1994) examined the progress of third graders over several years before and after the implementation of a single-track year-round calendar with optional intersession programs. "Although both the district and state experienced overall score decreases during these years, YRE students experienced less overall score decline" (p. 257). Academic results were mixed; for some subjects in some years, there was progress, whereas at other times, there was not. In addition, she found a "positive year-round impact on affective and social dimensions" (p. 257). Overall, she found that year-round school students experienced significantly lower levels of summer learning loss than their traditional counterparts.

There are several reports of strong parental support for single-track and dual-track or school-within-a-school calendars. Baker's thesis (1990) demonstrates strong support for a calendar change. In her study of Conroe Independent School District, she found that this support was associated with the opportunity for parental choice of either the traditional calendar or the alternative, "six-weeks-of-class followed by two-weeks-of-vacation schedule with an additional three-week summer vacation" (p. 21). In another study, Warrick-Harris (1995) chronicles the experience of a dual-track school that had enrolled around 310 students, most within walking distance of the school. Over a five-year period, escalating enrollment required a change. After examining the research into year-round schooling, the board decided to implement a school-within-a-school, with part of the school remaining on the August-June schedule and the others voluntarily opting for a 45-15 schedule with intersession. She found that the strong parental support for the revised calendar was associated with the opportunity for choice.

In general, most writers who advocate a re-examination of the school calendar to improve the educational opportunities for students are supportive of the single-track year-round calendar (Doyle & Finn, 1985; Perry, 1991). Some see it as a way of offering a longer school year, without necessarily changing the legislative mandate. Doyle and Finn, for example, suggest an optional fourth term; Perry recommends the "integration of summer school into the school year" (p. 11).

Although the wide-spread use of single-track year-round school is still a relatively new phenomenon, the literature is clear that those who are involved with it believe that it shows great promise. While the other common form of year-round calendar, multi-track year-round school (YRS), implemented to resolve overcrowding and population growth, is often associated with controversy, a single-track schedule seems to have few disadvantages and much potential to benefit both students and their families.

DISADVANTAGES AND ADVANTAGES OF SINGLE-TRACK YEAR-ROUND CALENDARS

In this chapter we have provided examples, illustrations, and vignettes, drawn from the YRS literature and our own research, to promote understanding of single- and dual-track year-round schooling. Here, in summary, are some of the ideas that are most frequently raised by respondents as disadvantages or advantages of these calendar modifications.

Disadvantages of Single-Track Year-Round Schooling

It should be noted that although a number of people raised some of the following issues as possible disadvantages, most indicated that they were perceptions or fears related to pre-implementation concerns that were not, in fact, borne out in practice following implementation of the single-track schedule. The primary concerns included:

- availability of childcare
- the need for and cost of air-conditioning in the summer
- conflicts with the more common district schedule
- facilitating building cleaning and repair
- children wanting to be on the same schedule as friends or relatives in other schools
- complexity of scheduling family vacations if children are in different schools on more than one schedule

Sometimes districts claim that costs and difficulties associated with air-conditioning and other considerations relating to facilities and district operations are the primary reasons for not implementing ST-YRS. In general, after implementation has occurred, the last two listed above are the most common enduring complaints. Children continue to want to be on the same schedule as their friends and there is little doubt that some families with children in schools with several different calendars find scheduling a challenge.

Advantages of Single-Track Schedules

To complete the picture of single-track year-round schooling, the following list represents some of the most commonly noted advantages reported by respondents.

- opportunities for intersession
- more regular visits to non-custodial parents
- time for teacher planning and reflection
- more motivation for both teachers and students
- reduced teacher burnout
- better attendance
- decreased vandalism
- fewer disciplinary referrals
- regular, extended preparation time for teachers
- assistance for those with health problems
- relief of both personal and interpersonal tensions
- more conversation and reflection about teaching and learning
- reduced summer learning loss
- a change in the organization of instructional units

Although all of the reported benefits are cited with regularity, perhaps most important are those with a direct impact on the learning experiences of children. These include reduced summer learning loss and intersession opportunities, increased teacher reflection and conversation about teaching and learning, as well as better planning and organization of instruction.

CONCLUSION

For the most part, people who have experienced single-track or community-based dual-track year-round schooling perceive it to be a highly desirable and effective calendar change. In fact, in our research in 34 districts in both the United States and Canada, we have rarely found anyone who would choose the traditional calendar over a single-track version.

In general, we have found that there are some obvious reasons why districts find ST-YRS to be a viable and advantageous option when they seek educational reform. Single-track YRS may be introduced into existing buildings with little increase in fiscal expenditures and with few requirements for additional materials, staff, or teachers. It appears to respond to the calls of researchers, such as Cooper and associates (1996), for reducing summer learning loss. When intersession is added, ST-YRS provides additional remediation or enrichment particularly to students who, by their attendance, voluntarily lengthen their school year.

Community-based approaches, in which the calendar is developed in consultation with members of the community to respond to their unique needs, are particularly effective. By increasing communication between the school and its wider community, the school is generally perceived to be more responsive and accessible. In turn, this often helps to build support for, and increase involvement in, school programs and activities.

Although often an end in itself, single-track YRS is also sometimes advantageous as a transition to multi-track year-round schooling. In addition, it frequently provides an impetus for continuing innovation and improvement to better meet the needs of students. Finally, as we shall see in Chapter 3, although single-track year-round schooling is effective and workable as an elementary school innovation, it is equally beneficial as a secondary school alternative (where its potential is just beginning to be explored and better understood).

We have found that for patrons and educators, who are discontented with the traditional school calendar, considering a single-track model may be one way to begin to break the status quo and to introduce changes that may have widespread benefits to a school-community.

CHAPTER 2:

MULTI-TRACK YEAR-ROUND SCHOOLING

In just three years, we got ourselves off the state's critically low list. Then, I got summoned to the state capital and I told them, "You told me to do it. You told me I could do it. And I did it and now you think I'm cheating." It wasn't all YRS, but that was certainly a big part of it. (Elementary school principal)

*****

When you have 950 elementary-school kids anyway, you have enough complications. Year-round to me just adds a whole other complication on top. If it's avoidable, it needs to be avoided. (Superintendent)

*****

In multi-track year-round schooling (MT-YRS), students are organized in classes on tracks with staggered schedules, with some being on vacation while others are in class. The difference between this and a single-track schedule is that not all students are in school at any one time. Typically, the students and their teachers are divided into three, four, or five groups, called tracks. At any given time, one of the tracks will be on vacation while the others are attending school. The schedules rotate, as demonstrated in Figures 2.1 and 2.2.

Usually introduced in an attempt to keep up with rapidly increasing enrollment, multi-tracking is an efficient way to accommodate more children in existing buildings. For instance, a school population of 800 students, on a traditional schedule, could be increased to 1000 students on a five-track schedule by rotating groups of 200 students and their teachers in and out of the building. As in single-track schedules, students usually spend the same amount of time in school as their peers on traditional schedules, with their in-class and vacation time distributed differently. Because space is more at a premium in multi-track schools, educators frequently have to be more creative if they also want to offer intersession programs.

The following comments are representative of the perceptions of parents from a number of different schools concerning the multi-track year-round schedule:

- Nine weeks on—three weeks off—avoids burnout. Three-week breaks are just right!
- I think the three week breaks are a distraction and it takes too much time to recover and get back to work on the YR system.
- I like year round. I've had kids in school on three different schedules. It gives me great one-on-one time when someone is off alone.
- It's hard to have community events when some kids are always in school.
- Multi-track keeps learning fresher.
- My son in junior high has commented that he misses it and wishes he still had the YR schedule.
- YRS weakens the family and, if you weaken the family, you obviously weaken the community.

These comments, drawn from our parent survey data, indicate that there is very little consensus concerning multi-track year-round schooling. Of all of the forms of modified school calendar, multi-track YRS is the most controversial. Where one family may like its flexibility for vacation planning and childcare arrangements and may believe it benefits children's learning, another finds that vacations and childcare are more difficult to schedule and that their children enjoy the long summer vacation without experiencing boredom.

Despite the controversial nature of multi-track year-round schooling, as of 1999 there were approximately 1,200 multi-track year-round schools in the United States and Canada. This represents roughly 40% of all year-round school calendars. A closer examination of some models of multi-track year-round schooling provides some understanding of the challenges and opportunities associated with this schedule.

A TYPICAL MULTI-TRACK MODEL OF YRS

In Chapter 1, a typical single-track 45-15 schedule was presented. One of the most common variations of the multi-track schedule, it uses an overlapping configuration to permit school buildings to house 33% more students than would be possible on a traditional calendar. In this version, shown in Figure 2.1, all students and teachers have a common three-week summer vacation. Two groups, or tracks, benefit from a six-week vacation. Track A ends earlier while track D begins later than the others and ensures, in these two cases, a six-week summer break. Tracks A, B, and C begin on the same date near the end of July. Following three weeks of schooling, track B moves to a three-week break, while track D begins its academic year. Looking at the schedule, you can see that at any given time, three tracks are in school, and one is on vacation. It is interesting to note that some teachers and students prefer tracks B or C, which offer long midwinter breaks around Christmas, to the more traditional A and D schedules.

The state from which this calendar was adopted has a legislative mandate for 180 days of school. For this particular model, to facilitate holidays and a common three-week summer break, the district received a waiver permitting it to extend each school day for multi-track schools by approximately 20 minutes and to shorten the number of school days per track to 170. Using this model, students and teachers fulfill the state-established time requirements for the academic year by putting in the same amount of time in a slightly different way.

This type of legislative waiver is not permitted in all jurisdictions. Thus, in some forms of the 45-15 calendar, there will not be a common summer vacation as each track's schedule is slightly prolonged. In other areas, decision makers have opted for a 60-20 calendar rather than the 45-15 schedule described above. There are also a number of other configurations of multi-track year-round schooling designed to meet the requirements of different districts and communities. For example, if more (or less) space than an additional 33% is required, a district may opt for five tracks permitting 25%

Figure 2.1   Multi-track 45–15 day calendar.

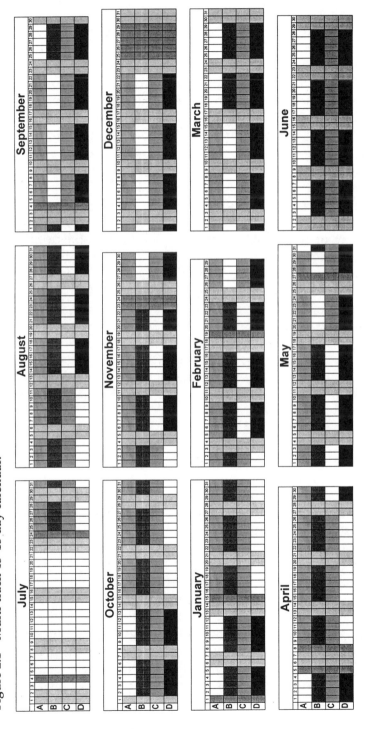

A, B, C, D = Tracks

more students or three tracks permitting 50% more students to be accommodated. Appendix A provides an overview of some of the most common multi-track plans and the amount of space that may be saved with each one.

Some multi-track calendars operate with overlapping tracks on less regular schedules than those already identified. Figure 2.2 shows one such schedule. In this district, because it is not possible to change the number of school days or the length of the day to accommodate a three-week summer vacation, the pattern of schooling and vacation is more irregular than for the 45-15 calendar. The common vacation time is reduced to 10 days with the pattern of in-school and vacation periods as shown. This demonstrates that the multi-track year-round schedule, although frequently similar from district to district, may also be modified to meet the needs of particular locales.

One other variation needs to be mentioned. In this modification, the teacher is given an extended contract and is available throughout an expanded academic year. Students in any given class are assigned a track and rotate in and out of the same classroom according to a schedule similar to the ones described above. However, in this model, at any given time, only 75% of the class is present. This schedule, sometimes known as the Orchard Plan, requires a great deal of flexibility and individualization of instruction on the part of classroom teachers.

INTERSESSION IN MULTI-TRACK SCHOOLS

Although it is easier to implement intersession programs in single-track schools, where the possibility of remediation or enrichment often provides the initial impetus for the calendar change, intersession may still be introduced in multi-track YRS. Because multi-tracking is generally implemented to resolve difficulties of space, the initial conceptualization does not always include thinking about ways to offer programming for students who are off-track. This frequently comes later as educators become aware of the potential benefits of providing learning opportunities for students on breaks. Sometimes multi-tracking alleviates overcrowding in schools enough to open areas that may be used for special activities. We found one MT school in Florida, in which intersession was planned

Figure 2.2 Irregular multi-track calendar.

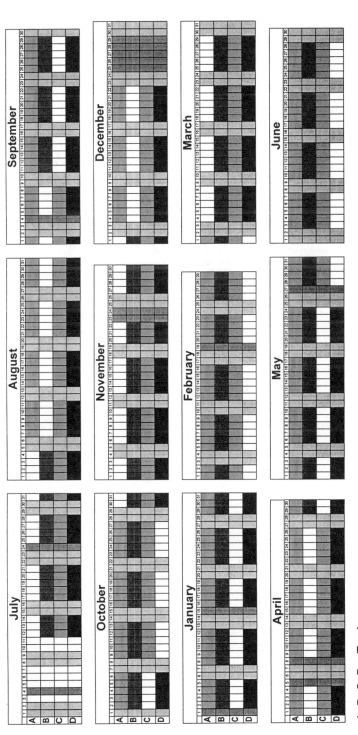

A, B, C, D = Tracks

from the outset. The staff at Jerico Elementary[1] demonstrated particularly creative use of educational programming for a MT calendar.

JERICO ELEMENTARY SCHOOL

When Esther was first assigned as a principal to Jerico Elementary School, she was faced with an older, under-resourced brick building with 28 portable classrooms and a poorly performing student body. Approximately 50% of the students were Hispanic, 33% were migrants, and many were non-English-speaking students or had limited English proficiency. This diversity, combined with unusually high levels of poverty and transience and low levels of parental involvement, added to Esther's challenges.

During her first year, she was faced with several dilemmas: how to move the school off Florida's list of "critically low" schools, how to meet the needs of the highly diverse and transient population, and how to best achieve the district mandate to implement multi-track year-round schooling. In this district, in any year in which a school exceeded its designated capacity by at least 20%, district policy required that the school principal begin community consultations and move to a multi-track schedule in the following year. Although this mandate had not been followed in more affluent areas of the district, Esther was required (and determined) to proceed.

Convinced that additional changes were needed to move her school out of the quagmire and to improve student learning, Esther arranged for teachers to travel in groups of two, four, or six to examine year-round schooling and other educational programs they might implement. Teachers soon realized that there would be two advantages to the year-round schedule. First, in conjunction with permission to build two new wings of eight classrooms each, the move to YRS significantly reduced the need for portables and increased access to playground equipment and school facilities. Second, the school could introduce some innovative and necessary intersession programs. As a result of their investigations, to better meet the needs of the school's 850 students, Esther's teachers chose to take training in two areas: instruction and parental involvement.

[1]The name, as others, is a pseudonym.

Several new programs were introduced to bring parents into the school. As an outgrowth of the teacher in-service, an attempt was made to welcome parents at all hours of every day and a regular newsletter was sent home in both English and Spanish. Pre-kindergarten classes were instituted and non-English-speaking parents were invited to learn common vocabulary words with their children. A high school equivalency (GED) tutoring program for parents was introduced on Monday and Wednesday evenings. On "Wonderful Wednesday," breakfast was served to both children and parents. On "Drive-Through-Friday," parents could drop off their kids, pick up a cold breakfast and an accompanying sheet of parenting tips. A "Make-and-Take" room was also established to permit parents to make educational materials to help their children at home. When one track was scheduled to return from vacation on the day of state SAT testing, parents were asked to help students practice test taking for an hour a day during the preceding week. Overall, parental involvement and support for the school dramatically improved during Esther's first three years.

Accompanying these efforts to include parents were many other educational innovations. In addition to a new academic emphasis with higher expectations for student performance, the staff instituted an uninterrupted 90-minute daily reading program to which children were assigned by reading level. Frequent monitoring of progress occurred to ensure appropriate development and placement. These efforts were supported by an after-school tutoring program conducted four days a week by certified teachers.

Intersession was developed as "Super-Session" and, until space could be found in the school, was originally held in the lounge of a nearby apartment complex. During each three-week period, 60 off-track students were identified by their teachers as being most in need of special programs (either remedial or enrichment). These students came, in groups of 20, during one of the three weeks of intersession to participate in an intensive program run by two para-professionals under the supervision of a classroom teacher and the Title 1[2] resource teacher. Some students came for several sessions a year; others requesting it were put on a waiting list, as the program proved popular with students and parents. Following the

[2]Title 1 is the name of a federally funded program in the United States that provides additional funding to support at-risk students.

completion of the new school wings, Super-Session was relocated in one of four remaining portables set aside for that purpose.

In her fourth year as principal, Esther was summoned to the state capital, with test scores, enrollment lists, and videos of the school in hand, to prove that her students' success was attributable to their improved achievement and not to some sleight of hand on her part. Esther attributed the school's success to a combination of her own hard work, the willingness of her staff to learn, increased parental involvement, and the fortuitous move to year-round schooling. The calendar change, she reported, not only facilitated some of the programming, in particular the Super-Sessions, but also helped her teachers to avoid burnout and to return to school following each three-week break refreshed and ready to offer their all to their students.

In Jerico School, it is clear that the combination of excellence in administration and teaching, flexibility and perseverance in pedagogy, and the impetus of an innovative calendar change, operated together to provide an improved educational program for the students. In other schools, in other areas, although the details are quite different, we see a similar combination of factors.

MOUNT SINAI SCHOOL

Mount Sinai Elementary School, in Missouri, has a long history of being on a year-round school schedule, sometimes single-track but most frequently multi-track. When the incumbent principal, Dr. Valerie Shipley, began her tenure ten years ago, the school was on a multi-track schedule. After her first four years, because of a temporary decline in student enrollment, the school moved to a single-track schedule. Although the presence of everyone in the building at the same time provided a welcome opportunity for the staff to interact as a whole, all were prepared to return to a multi-track schedule when enrollment increased. Indeed, after a couple of years, the school changed back in 1993 to the four-track calendar (tracks A, B, C, and D), which had previously been in effect.

In recent years, although the number of administrators remained the same—one principal and two assistant principals—the allocated duties, particularly those of the assistant principals, changed. Initially, the assistant principals were responsible horizontally, across all tracks for either grades K-3 or 4-6. When it became apparent that an increase of vertical integration might foster greater continuity for students and their parents and increased consistency from grades K-6, administrative assignments were changed. This resulted in one assistant principal assigned to tracks A and C and the other to tracks B and D. Valerie informed us that this "helps with curriculum discussion, it helps with parents, it helps because you know the kids from K-6." The new vertical integration, enthusiastically supported by the district, brought about a greater sense of the school as a whole and better understanding of individual students who could now be followed by the same administrator through their elementary school experience.

At the same time, another creative approach to scheduling enabled the school to maintain its horizontal integration. Prior to their two years on the single-track schedule (when everyone had been in the school at the same time), teachers had not been aware of the extent of their isolation. Their time on a single-track schedule had emphasized the need for better communication when they returned to a MT calendar. The staff, therefore, developed a six-day cycle and scheduled the specialist teachers (music, art, physical education) in order to permit a common planning time for each grade level across all tracks, regardless of the rotation. When we asked whether other district schools were also on the six-day schedule, we were told this was the only one and that they had "just figured it out" to increase teacher interaction across tracks. We were informed that the increased horizontal integration had resulted in more sharing of materials, better utilization of common spaces allocated to specific grade levels, and increased talk among teachers about teaching and learning, while the vertical integration helped ensure unity and consistency.

Soon after the school moved back to a multi-track schedule, the district instituted a middle school philosophy that involved the intended transfer of sixth graders to designated middle school buildings. However, because the policy preceded the capacity of middle schools to include all sixth graders, the sixth grade students at Mount Sinai were scheduled to wait for two years to actually attend a different building. Concerned about the delay for their students, Dr. Shipley and her teaching staff made the decision to implement a sixth grade middle school program within Mount Sinai

School. This involved two classes of sixth graders and two teachers who team taught. To facilitate this program, Valerie requested that the district remove a wall from one wing of the building. The renovated space then became the traditional calendar "middle school," within the existing multi-track school. For sixth graders, both the school day and the academic year were on the schedule adopted by the districts' middle schools, while the rest of the school continued its four-track rotating schedule. This innovation demonstrates that, at least for Valerie, the multi-track YR schedule was not so administratively challenging that it inhibited the possibility of additional educational innovations that might benefit the students.

When asked how she handled staff meetings and communication with some teachers on a multi-track schedule and others on the traditional middle school schedule, Valerie outlined an elaborate system of representative committees that, she said, actually conducted the business of the school. When she had previously attempted to make decisions with her 60 staff members present, it had been an unwieldy process she described as "a mob." She informed us that she conducted monthly staff meetings primarily for information, communicated on a daily basis with the teachers via email, and convened the committees as necessary. For example, at the budget committee, grade-level chair people, who were paid a stipend by the district for taking on additional responsibilities, made decisions concerning the allocation of school financial resources.

When we commented on the number of changes occurring at Mount Sinai School, Valerie shared her belief that the year-round schedule forces teachers to be more flexible. "There is something about having to move every nine weeks which makes you more organized and more ready to innovate."

The vignettes from these two schools were presented to give some of the flavor of how multi-track year-round schooling is implemented in areas that are quite different in terms of tradition, district support, and socioeconomic status. One demonstrates how multi-track schools may use intersession to change learning opportunities, while the other shows creative deployment of administrators to improve communications, unify the school, and promote continued innovation. Although MT-YRS is controversial and challenging in many areas, these vignettes are illustrations of its successful implementation.

We also visited a few MT schools in which the inherent social and political situations made YRS a much less successful or satisfying experience. This range of polarized opinions will be more fully explored in the second section of this book.

FISCAL ISSUES RELATED TO MULTI-TRACK YEAR-ROUND SCHOOLING

It is almost impossible to consider multi-track models of year-round schooling without mentioning financial issues. We introduce the topic briefly here but refer the reader to Chapter 10 for a more extensive discussion.

For multi-track schools, which are frequently implemented to relieve overcrowding, to alleviate the need to build new school facilities, or to redress shortfalls in capital outlays, several factors must be considered in determining accurate costs or benefits to a district. Although the overall operating costs of an individual school inevitably increase when it moves from a single-track or traditional-calendar program to multi-track, the costs per pupil across the district generally decrease. For this reason, long-term capital costs must be included in the calculation when assessing the financial impact of multi-track YRS. In most cases, the district savings in personnel and supplies decrease the average annual per pupil costs. Moreover, the savings may be substantial when the capital-cost benefits are factored in. Thus, multi-track year-round schooling permits districts to house more students in fewer buildings, reducing not only building costs but also the need for additional secretaries, caretakers, school administrators, and, in some cases, classroom teachers. Research indicates that fiscal benefits vary considerably by district, but that on a long-term basis, a district may accrue considerable savings by moving to a multi-track year-round school program.

It bears repeating that the savings realized through multi-track year-round schooling accrue at the district level rather than for individual schools where, with an increased number of students, operating costs will probably increase. Moreover, it is important to recognize that cost savings and educational quality are not incompatible. We have found that when carefully implemented, the year-round schedule may have educational benefits, act as a catalyst for additional innovation, and with some creativity, permit intersession offerings as well.

WHAT DOES THE LITERATURE SAY ABOUT MULTI-TRACK
YEAR-ROUND SCHOOLING?

As noted in Chapter 1, the literature on the effects of multi-track year-round (MT-YR) schooling can be somewhat confusing as it frequently fails to identify whether the calendar being discussed is a single-track or multi-track schedule. In some cases, there has been no attempt made to determine the similarity of year-round schools to schools in the comparison group. Another study did not take into consideration the differences in teachers—stable, experienced teachers on the one hand and a series of pre-service student teachers from the university on the other. Some studies have attempted to determine the impact of a calendar change during the first year of implementation (never a recommended strategy) despite the finding of a study conducted in New Jersey that "the benefits of year-round schooling did not become apparent until after four years of implementation" (cited in Merino, 1983, p. 303).

In general, because multi-track schools have sometimes been instituted by legislative mandate or forced on districts by demographic and fiscal considerations, there are often concomitant political pressures for early assessment of the success of the innovation. This need to be accountable to the electorate sometimes leads to misleading reports about the effectiveness, or lack thereof, of multi-track YRS.

Although the literature is vast, its usefulness and quality are mixed. Some reports (Hill, 1980; McDaniel, 1976; Sardo-Brown & Rooney, 1992), while valid research, focus on pre-implementation perceptions of respondents who never have experienced year-round schooling. In North Carolina, the largest systematic study of attitudes toward year-round schooling surveyed 2600 licensed drivers across the state (Carpenter, 1977) and found that most respondents were against a change in the school schedule. These articles accurately report very negative perceptions on the part of respondents; however, research is clear that once people have experienced a form of year-round schooling for more than one year, the acceptance rate is generally as high or higher than it was for the previous schedule in the same school (Russell, 1976; Zykowski et al., 1991).

Other research is less compelling because authors are selective in the data reported, often basing their findings on portions of newspaper or journal articles or district reports, without complete investigations to support the allegations. For example, Rasberry (1994) reports a news story that says, "school administrators in Davis District say they were sold a bill of goods . . . and would like to get back to the traditional schedule as soon as possible" (p. 17). She does not indicate that these comments were made specifically in response to a controversial one-year experiment at a junior high school. Her statement implies that all administrators in the district feel this way and ignores Davis District's decade-long commitment to year-round education, evidenced by the fact that almost one half of the district's elementary school students are being successfully educated in multi-track year-round schools. This information has also been reported regularly in local papers.

Another instance where some reports may be misleading is the case of Los Angeles Unified School District (LAUSD). Some articles (Taylor, 1993) imply that LAUSD has chosen to move away from year-round schooling. While over time, some schools have returned to a traditional schedule, as of 1998 the district maintained 218 schools, including 17 high schools, with 300,000 students on year-round schedules. In fact, in 1998, LAUSD was still the number one district in the United States as far as year-round schools were concerned, with both the greatest number of schools and highest number of elementary, junior high, and high school students, respectively, on the YR schedule.

Merino (1983), in an often-quoted article, examined 331 citations and based her research review on "well-designed studies . . . only those studies analyzing the impact of year-round schooling with a pre/post test design and a control group" (p. 314). Her meta-analysis found mixed results in terms of academic achievement, overall positive teacher attitudes toward year-round schooling, a general reduction in juvenile crime and delinquency for students enrolled in year-round schools, and no significant differences in participation in "extra-curricular activities, camps, vacation Bible schools, or [teachers'] graduate study" (p. 313).

More recently, Zykowski and associates (1991) described a number of aspects of year-round schooling in California. The study covered issues related to costs, academic achievement, and perceptions of teachers, parents, and the community. Kneese (1996) provided an updated meta-analysis based on rigid criteria similar to those used by Merino. Each of these studies reported generally positive responses on the part of people with experience with YR calendars as well as a moderate positive impact on students' academic achievement.

The following studies focused on specific aspects of the multi-track year-round calendar. Christie (1989) compared the impact of the Concept 6 plan with other YR calendars and the traditional calendar on instructional quality, work life, and student outcomes. She concluded that all of the schedules were approximately equal in terms of what they offered teachers and students. Herman (1991) found that parents and students were moderately in favor of YRS after implementation, whereas teachers and administrators believed students learned more and experienced less fatigue on the YRS schedule than on the traditional calendar. Gandara and Fish (1994) summarized the impact of the Orchard Plan in several schools and found teachers surprisingly positive about the within-class rotation of students. Mutchler (1993) found, in her study of third grade students in San Diego, that students in multi-track year-round schools performed better on reading tests than students in either single-track or traditional-calendar schools.

Weinert (1987) focused on structure modifications such as teacher planning areas that enhance the effectiveness of multi-track year-round schooling. Gandara (1992) identified increased opportunities for teachers to extend their contracts in year-round schools. Quinlan, George, and Emmett (1987) compared traditional and YR schools and generally found little difference in their academic performance. They further asserted that where inner-city schools on YR schedules performed at a slightly lower level than other schools in the study, this was not attributable to the YR calendar but to other factors related to inner-city populations. An article by Donato (1996) described the negative impact of implementing the multi-track year-round calendar in a district that did not take into consideration the effect on the (predominantly Mexican-American) population of migrant farm workers.

A group of articles provides analyses of costs and benefits associated with multi-track schooling (Baker et al., 1978; Brekke, 1985; Denton & Walenta, 1993; Hazelton et al., 1992; Hough et al., 1990). The analyses support the fiscal viability of YRS and are discussed in Chapter 10.

The foregoing summary is an overview intended to give the flavor of the research on multi-track year-round schooling. It is in no way a complete or comprehensive literature review. Although the quality and utility of individual articles vary, in its totality the literature gives a clear picture of the complexity, the difficulties, and the opportunities associated with multi-track year-round schooling.

DISADVANTAGES AND ADVANTAGES OF MULTI-TRACK YEAR-ROUND CALENDARS

Here are some of the ideas that are most frequently raised by respondents as disadvantages or advantages of MT-YRS.

Disadvantages of Multi-Track Year-Round Calendars

The primary concerns, compiled from our surveys and interviews of administrators, parents, and teachers, include the following. It is worth noting that some of these are pre-implementation concerns that often dissipate following implementation.

- complexity of scheduling family vacations if children are on more than one schedule, for example, junior or senior high school
- availability and difficulty of obtaining childcare
- the need for and cost of air-conditioning in the summer
- conflicts with other district schedules
- building cleaning and repair while students are in class
- children wanting to be on same schedule as friends or relatives
- time lost for track change activities
- teacher movement of supplies and sharing of resources
- administrator burnout
- controversy concerning track assignments
- potential for inequities in track assignments
- ghettoization of certain groups by track
- difficulty for community in knowing whether children are truant
- concern about fracturing neighborhood identity
- difficulty of staff communication
- concerns about loss of school identity

Benefits of Multi-Track Schedules

To complete the picture of multi-track year-round schooling, the following list represents some of the most commonly noted advantages reported by our respondents.

- opportunities for intersession
- regular opportunities to visit non-custodial parents
- time for teacher planning and reflection
- better motivation for both teachers and students
- less teacher burnout
- better attendance (student and teacher)
- reduced vandalism
- fewer disciplinary referrals
- preparation time for first-year teachers
- assistance for those with health problems
- relief of stress
- reduction of conflict and tensions (among students and staff)
- more conversation and reflection about teaching and learning
- better year-round use of facility
- accommodation of more students in buildings
- greater student access to equipment and facilities
- teacher mobility and sharing of resources
- teacher communication and team teaching of units
- availability of off-track teachers as qualified substitutes
- increased community involvement
- improved parental participation
- promotion of more focused units of instruction
- perception of the extended school year as more "professional"

CONCLUDING COMMENT

We have seen that multi-track year-round school calendars are generally introduced to address fiscal concerns related to overcrowding. Perhaps the general perception that the MT schedule is as much a political and fiscal issue as an educational reform helps to explain why MT-YRS is the most controversial (although not the most prevalent) year-round schedule.

Most overcrowded schools are found in large urban areas where some of the difficulties inherent in inner-city schools are often confounded with year-round schooling issues. Sometimes people reject MT-YRS, arguing that effecting fiscal savings without proof of academic improvement is an inadequate reason for educational change. Yet, we have found no evidence, either in our research or in the literature, to suggest that MT-YRS have a negative impact on student learning. In fact, given the often deteriorating social and economic conditions in inner cities, the common finding of "no difference" between the academic outcomes of traditional and multi-track schools may actually be very promising. It suggests that the calendar change has provided a way for student achievement to be maintained in over-crowded schools at a level comparable to traditional calendar schools elsewhere.

There is little doubt that a year-round schedule presents particular administrative challenges and requires strong and effective leaders who are able to deal with mixed parental responses to the calendar, handle the complexity of a rotating schedule, and engage in effective communications with the community as well as the district. However, where MT-YRS is implemented without adequate support and leadership and without due consideration of the additional political, social, and fiscal issues that will be examined in Section 3, it may be an unmitigated disaster.

In our experience, multi-track year-round schooling has the potential to combine fiscal efficiency with educational excellence. Where implemented with creativity, strong leadership, and commitment, it can provide the impetus for additional innovations that have the capability to improve student learning.

Our discussion in these first two chapters of single-track and multi-track calendars has related specifically to elementary schools that constitute, by far, the greatest percentage of modified-calendar schools. Nevertheless, we do not want to leave the impression that year-round schooling is only an elementary school phenomenon. In the next chapter we examine some of its modifications and adaptations for use at the secondary level—both junior high and senior secondary schools.

CHAPTER 3:

YEAR-ROUND SCHOOLING AT THE
SECONDARY LEVEL

We went into it from an educational perspective, and we thought that we could, perhaps, initiate some real systemic reform if we toppled the agrarian calendar. The research at the time said that it was much better in terms of cutting down on the time for review, and retention was better, but most of that stuff, you know, was in the elementary level. (Secondary school teacher)

*****

The counselors get hammered. The clerical staff gets hammered, so what you end up doing is you end up really hurting the leadership and the management. The teachers—it's a piece of cake. I mean, it's great! (Superintendent)

*****

I want to know what on earth is going on in this school. Traditionally, we get called to schools in this area of the city almost daily and now you don't ever seem to need me. (Police liaison officer)

*****

Secondary schools are generally considered to be more complex and more resistant to change than elementary schools; hence, there is a popular belief that year-round schooling may not be a workable innovation at the secondary school level. Nevertheless, numerous forms of year-round schooling have been tried, with varying degrees of success, in secondary schools across North America. In all, as of 1998, there were 273 junior high and middle schools with approximately 260,000 students and 203 high schools with 180,500 students participating in year-round schooling.

The multi-track (MT) model most frequently found at the secondary level seems to be the Concept 6 approach, which is basically a three-track, rotating calendar. This form of multi-track year-round schooling seems to work well in very large high schools. However, there are several issues that make implementing multi-track schedules in secondary schools difficult, foremost of which is scheduling. Assigning students to rotating tracks within a multi-track secondary school may become problematic. In general, high schools need to offer numerous subjects to prepare students for college and university as well as for various employment and career opportunities. Although some of these courses are very popular and widely subscribed, others have limited enrollment and are generally offered in single sections (sometimes called *singletons*) each term. In a large school, most subjects can be offered on more than one track. In a smaller school, operating on a multi-track schedule, students wanting senior college preparatory classes (such as a foreign language, calculus, physics, or computer science) might all have to be assigned the same track. This could necessitate scheduling of other classes, such as vocational electives, on a different track, thus restricting student options. It could also have the dangerous and inequitable effect of streaming the high school by track. Multi-track year-round schedules are not an easy option for many secondary schools wanting to effect a calendar change. There are, however, some exceptions.

One modification of the MT-YRS calendar appropriate for the secondary level is the Orchard Plan. In this plan, unlike in multi-track approaches, students rotate in and out of classrooms every 15 days in small groups of about seven students. Teachers teach for approximately 225 days on an extended contract, still enjoy eight weeks of vacation, and retain their own rooms. Under this plan, roughly 35 students are assigned to each class, but only 28 are in attendance at any one time. It is obvious that this calendar only works where there is considerable teacher flexibility and ability to individualize instruction.

If there is willingness to reinvest some of the cost savings accomplished by accommodating more students in a given building, it is possible to have a successful multi-track schedule in a smaller school by creative scheduling of singleton classes. For instance, permitting smaller than average classes to run on several tracks, at least in alternating years, is one solution. Although this will involve additional costs, the attendant advantages may justify the expenditure. Another option is to run a small offering, for example, a combined eleventh and twelfth grade French class on every track. This would permit all students to have access to the elective and help to avoid the danger of ghettoization mentioned earlier. It is also possible, where there is more than one high school on a MT-YR schedule, to offer electives so that students have increased access by traveling between schools.

MT-YRS is also an appropriate solution for schools (whether called junior high or middle school) that operate on a middle school philosophy of keeping groups of students together to enhance the cohesiveness of their educational program and the intimacy of their contacts with teachers. These principles can help to eliminate the problems of scheduling and to overcome inequitable track assignments. We describe a junior high school five-track model later in this chapter.

In general, however, it is the single-track modified schedule that seems to hold the most promise and to offer the most exciting possibilities at the secondary level. In fact, although in many places the potential of the ST-YR calendar is just beginning to be understood and studied, it may ultimately offer more opportunity for student success than its elementary counterpart. For these reasons, our discussion of high school or senior secondary school models in this chapter emphasizes the single-track schedule. Throughout the discussion, we stress the principle of calendar creation rather than calendar selection as a basis for effective secondary school models.

Before moving to a detailed examination of some of the models, the following comments, drawn from our surveys and interviews, will give a better flavor of the range of participant perceptions concerning YRS at the secondary level.

When you're getting so sick of school that you just want to quit, you get a break, and then it's not so bad. And then you come back, and it's like starting school all over again. It keeps you from, I don't know, hating school so much, and if you have a better attitude about school, it's easier to learn. (Student)

*****

The reason I like year round school better—a lot better—well, the big positive that cancels out all the little negatives, like sports—is intersession because, how could anything get better than intersession. (Student)

*****

As a guidance counselor I was DYING for an experience that was year round. I couldn't imagine how anybody wouldn't want it because of the opportunity to just recharge your batteries if nothing else. (Counselor)

*****

Well, the teachers and students may like it, but we don't. I have to run the programs to get ready for the report card time; plus, at the same time I have to start building the catalog and the master schedule for the intersession, and then you've got kids registering at the end of the nine weeks. It seems like you never get through with registration so that you can get down to the nitty gritty of running the school. (Secretary)

*****

Intersession costs? If you look at the bang for the buck, I don't think you can beat what we gave them. (Superintendent)

*****

Do we mind being the only YR high school in the district? Shhh! Don't tell anyone. We really enjoy the peace and quiet when nobody else is open. It's about focus, focus, focus. (Principal)

*****

These comments suggest that educators and students believe there are significant benefits associated with a year-round calendar, although some support staff believe that it adds considerably to their workload. Generally, where ST modified calendars in secondary schools are successful, they are accompanied by significant changes in the way the curriculum is organized. It is these modifications that appear to garner widespread support from students, parents, and educators. They are described in the following discussions of both a MT junior high and a ST senior high school model.

MULTI-TRACK JUNIOR-HIGH SCHOOL MODELS

In this section, we describe Stephen Lewis Junior High School[1], a seventh through ninth grade junior high school that has successfully implemented a 60-15 five-track schedule. We also describe two alternate experiences with the YR calendar at the junior high and middle school level, one reasonably successful and the other less so.

Stephen Lewis Junior High School

Interestingly, although year-round schooling has been slow to develop in Canada as a whole, Canada's first multi-track year-round school opened at a secondary level. In 1995, a five-track junior high school in Alberta began to draw international attention. In this case, when the district recognized the need to place a new school in a rapidly growing area of the city, it also made the decision to invest funds to design a building that would be conducive to alternative educational programming and be cost-effective in terms of housing more students than traditional schools. The resultant building was designed specifically for a YRS schedule and was built with four pods clustered around a central core. When a track returns from its break, the whole group enters the pod vacated by the departing track.

Stephen Lewis is a five-track junior high school whose approximately 1000-member student body is quite diverse. Opened in 1994, the school was built in a community with rapidly changing demographics, generally low socioeconomic status (SES), and associated social problems such as unemployment, crime, and youth violence. Because students had previously been bussed out of their neighborhood and dispersed among existing schools in other parts of the city, there had been no real junior high community in the area. As a result, the new school quickly took on a considerable level of importance as a focal point for community activities.

The schedule adopted by Stephen Lewis Junior High School is shown in Figure 3.1. You will note that, in the year shown, four of the five tracks (red, blue, green, and purple, representing approxi-

[1]The names here, as previously, are pseudonyms.

Figure 3.1 Five-track secondary calendar.

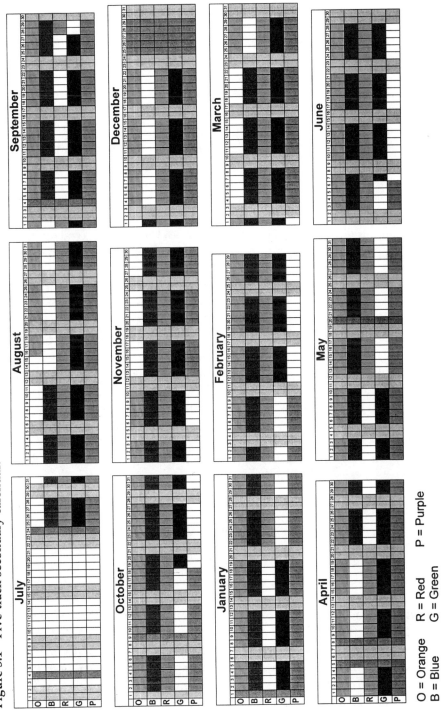

O = Orange   R = Red   P = Purple
B = Blue   G = Green

mately 80% of the school's population) began school on July 22. All had a vacation for the August holiday weekend. On August 12, the blue track (B) resumed its vacation until September 5, while the orange track (O) began a term that lasted until October 26. All students had a common Christmas vacation period between December 21 and January 5 and all shared summer vacation between June 27 and July 21. Students in the orange (O) and purple (P) tracks had longer summer vacations, the orange track because it started later than the others and the purple track because, for its students, classes had ended on June 5.

The principal, Naomi St. John, had been appointed 18 months prior to the opening of the school and had been released from her educational duties in her previous school for a period of six months to prepare for the opening of the new school. Given that this was the first alternative calendar school in the district, she argued successfully for a change in the traditional administrative allocation and was permitted to hire five learning leaders—one for each track—in place of the assistant principals normally provided for by the district contract. These learning leaders were teachers who were also appointed prior to the school opening. After a hard fought battle by the new principal, these learning leaders were also given some released time to engage in the planning and development of a shared school philosophy, assist with teacher hiring, and oversee specific aspects of the school's construction and equipment. The teachers were also given five days of released time to facilitate planning for instruction at the new school. Two organizational features reflecting a reconceptualization of teaching and learning grew from this planning and had an obvious impact on the students in Stephen Lewis School.

The first of these was the concept of learning communities. Each track was organized as a learning community based on some agreed-upon educational principles. In each learning community, four classroom teachers, a resource teacher, and the learning leader planned for the overall experiences of approximately 120 students who stayed in the community for their three years in the school. Although they did not have regularly assigned instructional duties, learning leaders assisted with instruction, worked with students individually, dealt with discipline, and provided key leadership and support roles in determining how educational experiences were organized and offered within each track. To meet the needs of the students, many of whom were designated as high risk, one teacher assigned to each community had a strong background in special education, while the others brought strengths in various subject areas.

The school day was organized in a series of flexible groupings: some were grade-level groupings and others were multi-age or cross-grade; some were ability groups (primarily for skill acquisition) and others were cross-ability heterogeneous groups (for cooperative learning or project-related activities). Sometimes students were grouped in large, combined classes with one teacher; at other times they worked with a teacher in very small groups or on a one-on-one basis. Within the learning community, students were taught the core academic subjects, optional elective classes, and participated in a teacher advisory program.

Despite the school's designation as a junior high school, the approach to instruction was both thematic and integrated, really more of a middle school approach than a discretely organized junior high school. In all of the school activities, the emphasis was on students taking increasing responsibility for their own learning, including peer and self-assessment. As each learning period ended, a celebration of learning was held during which parents were invited to come to the school to talk with teachers and students about their children's achievements and to attend student performances and presentations.

The second organizational feature that had an impact on student learning experiences at Stephen Lewis Junior High School was the "rainbow track"[2] unit, located in the central core of the building. This served all of the rotating tracks with three-week units of activities such as art, music, computing, drama, physical education, and home economics. When students of a learning community were engaged in these activities, their teachers used the common planning time for meetings and discussion of curricular issues.

To support a sense of being part of the school as a whole as well as of belonging to a smaller internal learning community, weekly staff meetings were held. Each month three of these meetings focused directly on matters related to teaching and learning, and the fourth was for business and information purposes. There was an

---

[2]Rainbow track is the name given to the schedule used by teachers whose duties cut across all of the tracks in the school designated by color, hence rainbow.

additional complex system of committees that included representation from each track, as well as parents and students. Committees discussed and recommended policy related to various aspects
of school life: governance, assessment and reporting, professional
development, and curriculum. Each committee chose two teacher
leaders to ensure that no matter what group was off-track, there
would be a leader present at meetings. Although this committee
structure ensured voice and representation, it was also time-con-
suming and somewhat cumbersome. Hence, although the new governance structure was perceived to be one of the strengths of the
school, it was also a source of major frustration, requiring a change
of mind-set on the part of the teachers.

Overall, the year-round schedule of Stephen Lewis School
remained very much in the background of the daily life of students
and teachers; nevertheless, there was a strong sense that this
structure facilitated and enhanced the opportunity to offer a re-
conceptualized curriculum to students. Despite the fact that many
changes might have occurred within a traditional schedule, in this
district, policy would not have allowed the structure of learning
leaders without the prior institution of a multi-track schedule. With
a more traditional approach to leadership, many of the curricular
changes, as well as the degree of teacher leadership, certainly would
not have occurred and would have been unlikely to continue.

ALTERNATIVE JUNIOR HIGH SCHOOL APPROACHES

Some jurisdictions in California organize into separate elementary
and secondary school districts. St. Michael School District is a secondary district, with some schools on MT-YR schedules and others on a traditional calendar. Its junior high multi-track schedule is
similar to that shown in Figure 2.2. In addition to a common two-
week vacation in July and an additional week at Christmas, all
tracks profit from numerous breaks during the year for statutory
holidays as well as nine additional days for teacher preparation or
in-service.

Another innovation in this district is a concept they call *villages*.
Villages are groups of approximately 200 students and teams of six
teachers, with each teacher responsible for a different subject area.
In addition to learning from their team of teachers, students rotate

through a number of eight-week optional or *exploration subjects* such as art. The band teacher, however, is scheduled as a *rainbow teacher*, requiring that students commit to band for the whole year, rather than any of the other exploration subjects. The intent of the village organization is to ensure that students find an affiliation (within a relatively large school) with a smaller group of students and teachers. The village concept is, however, difficult to schedule because the school has the additional challenge of incorporating both ESL and honors classes into its timetable.

It is interesting that the innovative village concept begun in multi-track schools has been extended into the district's traditional-calendar high schools. This provides an illustration of how innovation related to one reform initiative may have a secondary impact on other schools within a district.

In another Western state, a short-lived experiment with a multi-track schedule in a junior high school failed, in part, because the school maintained its secondary school approach to curriculum rather than change to the middle school concept that seems so successful in a MT environment at the junior high school level. This school opted for the 45-15 schedule (shown in Chapter 2, Figure 2.1) to accommodate its 1000 member student body. Using a seven-period school day, the staff allocated certain subjects, for example, French, band, and advanced art, to single tracks. Because electives are relatively limited in junior high school programs in this state, scheduling became a nightmare as students clamored for the tracks on which their preferred options were offered. Additional difficulties were posed by having students in physical education classes on one track wanting to participate in sports offered only by teachers on other tracks. To compound the problems in this school, parents were promised that if they had elementary school children on a specific track in a MT-YRS, their junior high school children could also be assigned to the same track—a promise that turned out to be impossible to fulfill.

During the first year of implementation, everyone involved with the experiment indicated that they had done what they had set out to accomplish; they had demonstrated that multi-track year-round schooling was workable, although not necessarily desirable, at the secondary level. This set the stage for a return, in the following year, to a traditional calendar.

A number of mitigating factors should be noted. Educators in this school persisted with the traditional subject and course organization and did not take advantage of the new calendar to modify the delivery of instruction or to offer an intersession program. If there had been better dissemination of information concerning year-round schooling at the secondary level, the experiment might have been more successful. Finally, the generally negative political climate within which the experiment was attempted almost certainly contributed to its failure.

As previously noted, multi-track schedules tend to work best at the secondary level if one or more of the following conditions exist: a large student body, an ability to offer curriculum in innovative ways (for example, in three-week modules), creative uses of intersession periods, or a philosophy (for example, a middle school approach) that supports the organization of students in clusters, villages, or communities. In fact, as more of these conditions are met, the likelihood of successful implementation increases. None of these conditions was present, however, in the latter experiment with multi-track year-round schooling.

SECONDARY SCHOOL SINGLE-TRACK YEAR-ROUND CALENDARS

Single-track schedules may offer flexible and creative ways to meet the needs of many secondary school students. The portrait of Persephone High School is presented to promote understanding of one school's experience with YRS as well as to prompt reflection on how the calendar may be adapted to address unique needs elsewhere.

Persephone High School

The faculty of Persephone High School, in the American Southwest, had been seeking a way to initiate some systemic reform to better serve the needs of its students. With approximately 1400 students and about 84 teachers, Persephone High School had the most multicultural student body in the district. Approximately 50% of the students were Caucasian, about 24% were Hispanic, 20% African-

American, with Asian-Pacific Islanders and Native American students making up the rest.

In the first half of the 1990s, Persephone High School experienced relatively low test scores accompanied by the lowest graduation rate and the highest dropout rate of any school in its district. To rectify this situation, an ad hoc group of interested teachers began a quest to determine how to implement changes that would address these problems and offer better educational opportunities to their students. Following an extensive period of study and discussion among themselves, and despite the fact that they had found a dearth of information regarding secondary school calendar reform, the group recommended to the staff that they seek approval to move to a single-track year-round school calendar. Following a vote of teachers and non-teaching staff, the school adopted the single-track schedule shown in Figure 3.2.

In general, the school followed the 45-15 calendar described in Chapters 1 and 2. As was the case for elementary schools that used this schedule, students began school in August and were compensated by having vacation periods distributed throughout the school year, with a final six-week summer vacation beginning at the same time as the other schools in the district.

To increase the flexibility of student offerings, Persephone replaced its semester system with a quarter system to support the implementation of the single-track calendar. The division of the academic year into quarters was one of two modifications associated with the adoption of their new calendar that created a number of exciting opportunities for students; the other was the institution of an extensive intersession program.

The move to a quarter system for assigning credits offered students increased opportunities to gain credits. Those who dropped out of school for any reason during one quarter were still able to gain credit for classes taken during the other three quarters. Shortening the attendance period required for attaining a credit improved the motivation of students who tended to begin each new term with renewed enthusiasm but who appeared unable to maintain the momentum for a whole semester. Of course, the introduction of a quarter system is not necessarily tied to the implementation of a year-round school calendar, but in this case, because of the intersession program, it was an integral part of the

Figure 3.2   Secondary single-track calendar.

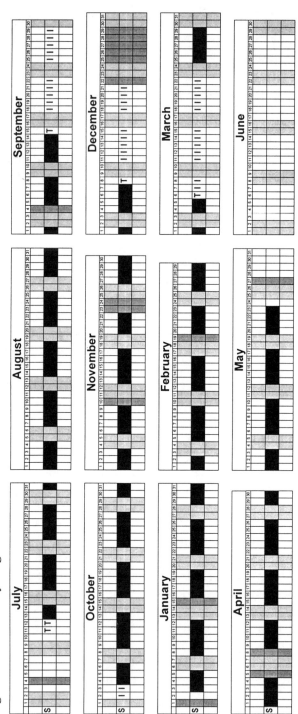

S = Single-track
T= Teacher only days
I = Intersession

reconceptualization of how to offer curriculum in ways that would enhance student opportunities for learning.

The intersession classes ran for the first two weeks of the three-week breaks between quarters and offered classes for four hours a day. This provided 40 hours of "seat time" per quarter credit. The staff took advantage of the intersession period to offer remediation, enrichment, or acceleration. Students might, therefore, complete courses in which they had been falling behind, retake classes that they had failed, or enroll in enrichment or acceleration options. Enrichment courses (for example, creating an internet web page, fly fishing, rock climbing, or business orientation classes) were considered to be noncredit courses but were posted to transcripts to indicate that students had profited from experiences they might not otherwise have had. Accelerated credits were given for classes that students could take as part of their regular program but that they elected to take during intersession. This expedited early graduation or opened up room in a student's schedule for an elective that otherwise might be in conflict with a required class.

The math department took advantage of this arrangement to require students who had failed an algebra class to retake it during intersession and to register for its sequel during the next regular quarter. In addition, the math department developed a popular way for students to take geometry as well as the algebra classes required for college entrance. Students took two quarter credits in geometry during the intersessions each year. Then, to complete the credit, they enrolled in a special one-month half-credit in geometry offered in June.

The English department spent considerable time working out a complex and comprehensive matrix of intersession offerings described by one of the school's guidance counselors as "phenomenal." Remedial classes in freshman English were offered during each intersession to ensure acquisition of basic skills. Teachers also offered a series of courses on a rotational basis: composition and creative writing classes (short story, poetry, and drama) that satisfied the requirements for almost any quarter of sophomore, junior, or senior English credit.

Other types of activities also occurred during intersession. Some examples include band, yearbook camps, and student council retreats. One teacher offered a "little theater" program that took performances to elementary schools during the intersession period.

Some teachers also profited from the intersession to visit other schools to observe teachers and learn about their programs. The extensive and innovative intersession offerings made a positive difference in student performance and achievement at Persephone High School. School officials reported that, on average, 30% of the students earned either a remedial or accelerated quarter credit each intersession, with an additional 4-7% earning enrichment credits. Overall, during the first two years of the year-round schedule, the dropout rate declined slightly. Both the number of students graduating and the number of credits achieved showed a small but gratifying increase.

ADAPTING THE MODEL

One high school in eastern Canada began to examine how it might adapt the model used by Persephone High School to its own unique situation. Like Persephone High School, this school has a multicultural student population, extremely low test scores, high dropout rates, low graduation and completion rates, and other issues related to student tensions and occasional violence.

When teachers of Glendale High School learned of the Persephone model, many were immediately interested. Here, it seemed, might be a way to give teachers and students breaks that would relieve some of the tensions, increase motivation, achieve a higher rate of course completion and graduation, and offer its own variations on the intersession program. Teachers began to explore how they could use the student teachers (on-site during the university semester) to offer intense skill-building intersession courses with a low student-to-adult ratio to raise the reading levels of many of the students. In addition, they thought students might be able to receive co-op or work-education credits for working as tutors in elementary schools during intersessions—giving them an opportunity to improve their own reading skills as well as those of the elementary students they were tutoring.

There were multiple variations—apparently limited only by the teachers' creativity—but the planning began to falter as they realized that to institute such a program with three-week breaks following completed academic quarters, they would have to start school at the beginning of August. In this area, where fishing has traditionally been important to the economy and where all schools are in session until the end of June, a late July or early August start seemed impossible. There would be no way to achieve buy-in from most of the teachers, let alone the parent and student population.

As teachers began to reflect on what was important about the proposed calendar modification, the three-week breaks with inter-session capabilities following the first and third quarters of academic work seemed particularly promising. In other words, following the second quarter, which could be considered similar to the turn around time between semesters, they were willing to proceed without intersession programs. Using this approach, they identified the number of minutes per day and then per year that the jurisdiction required students to be in class. By proposing a slightly longer school day, teachers were able to create the calendar shown in Figure 3.3.

In the proposed calendar, the first and third quarters would be followed by three-week breaks. Quarter two would be interrupted (as it was under their current calendar) by the Christmas vacation. School would end following the fourth quarter, before the end of June—at the same time as other schools in the area. And, best of all, this could be accomplished by starting school in the middle of August, a timeline that was likely to be acceptable to the school community.

As we went to press, Glendale school had not yet made its decision about whether to proceed. However, this example demonstrates that year-round schooling is a concept rather than a program. It is adaptable to specific situations, both at the elementary and the secondary school level, and it is most effective when it takes local conditions, norms, expectations, and requirements into consideration.

WHAT DOES THE LITERATURE SAY ABOUT YRS AT A SECONDARY LEVEL?

Although there are some districts in which large, multi-track secondary schools exist successfully, most of the existing programs and the majority of the literature relate to single-track forms of year-

Figure 3.3 Proposed secondary calendar.

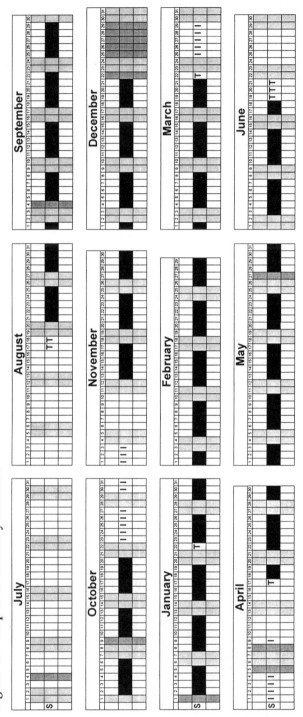

S = Single-track
T = Teacher only days
I = Intersession

round schooling. Many of the reviews of year-round secondary school experiences recount implementation that occurred during the 1970s.

From the literature, it appears that implementation during this period was often problematic. For example, Merino's review (1983) includes the following studies of high schools in which the authors did not find positive gains for year-round schedules. Matty (1978) found no difference for students of Hispanic background, but generally lower overall math scores in year-round than in traditional ninth grade classes. Ricketts (1976) compared achievement in junior high schools and found mixed results, although it appeared that vocabulary results favored students in year-round schools, whereas in algebra and geometry, students from traditional schools fared better. Deason (1975) found that the majority of 261 high school teachers were dissatisfied with multi-tracking and Webb (1973) learned that some teachers were positive towards the financial benefits of year-round schooling but that they also believed that YRS had a negative impact on their professional opportunities. In sum, Merino concluded that multi-track schedules in secondary schools appeared to be particularly disruptive to school routines (p. 313).

There are also a number of studies of secondary schools (including junior high school and middle schools) that require careful and cautious reading. As an example, Young and Berger (1983) assessed the experience of two Washington State junior high schools that had been on multi-track schedules. In part, they interviewed ninth grade students in year-round schools, as well as senior high school students who had previously experienced the junior high calendar, and a sample of parents and educators both in the district and in a matched comparison district. Seventy percent of respondents believed the "educational quality of year-round schools had been as good as in other districts on a nine month schedule" (p. 56). In a report such as this, much is left unsaid, because we have no way of knowing how respondents had perceived the quality of their previous calendar or the basis for the comparison of their district to the neighboring one.

Another unpublished study of a multi-track junior high school's experience should also be read with great caution (Greenwell et al., 1993). During the first year of implementation, approximately 1200 surveys were sent to parents in the first week of March. Of the 97 surveys returned (8% of the total), 62% or approximately 60 people were dissatisfied with the year-round school experiment. Despite the fact that this constituted only 5% of the school population (which may or may not have been representative) and despite a number of written comments in favor of continuing the experiment, the surveys were used to lobby the district to permit a return to the traditional calendar.

Many other recent studies of secondary YRS experiences provide evidence that implementing a YRS calendar is accompanied by a decrease of student dropout rates, an increase in graduation rates, an increased number of academic courses passed, and in general, better overall performance (Bradford, 1993; LAUSD, 1983, 1986; Peltier, 1991; White, 1987, 1988).

In Buena Vista District, in Virginia, a change to a four-quarter alternative calendar was made in 1974. There, the 60 day, three quarter, high school schedule had been supplemented by a somewhat voluntary fourth summer quarter. More than 50% of the regular day students attended the fourth quarter, with the distribution being roughly equal between courses taken for remediation and those for enrichment or extra credit. In 1990, each Virginia school division was given the authority to mandate fourth quarter attendance for all students whose test scores fell below the 25th percentile. In addition, "students from neighboring school divisions attend the fourth quarter in the summer to earn academic credit" (Virginia State Department, 1992, p. 54). Results reported by Bradford (1996) for a 20 year follow-up evaluation study of fourth quarter attendance suggested that the dropout rate of the district fell below the state average and that pupil achievement scores increased to a level equal to or greater than the national average.

Winters (1995) summarized the results of school and district tests reported for secondary schools in several states. Scores for Sweetwater High School, California, were mixed, with some scores statistically higher for year-round schools than for traditional schools in one year but with the opposite results reported for other years. Winters reported that in El Paso, Texas, most year-round schools achieved positive test results in reading, writing, and math. He stated that although "the district perceives that the YR program contributes to the recent success, school officials are quick to add that there are certainly many other variables to be considered" (p. 26).

Our own observations and interviews support the contention that when secondary school reform permits modification of the typical organizational structure to provide students with additional opportunities for remediation, academic credit, and enrichment, it can, indeed, be very effective. Many of these schools, such as Persephone and Stephen Lewis, have excellent and extensive internal program descriptions and evaluative materials; unfortunately, most of these have not been published and are not generally accessible. We hope they will soon be available to supplement the current, meager, and somewhat spotty, literature on year-round secondary schools.

DISADVANTAGES AND BENEFITS OF YR CALENDARS FOR SECONDARY SCHOOLS

The discussion concerning multi-track models at the secondary school level suggests that the disadvantages and benefits are similar to those outlined in Chapter 2. In general, they are not repeated here. However, we do signal the potential disadvantage of trying to offer a multi-track schedule in a high school that is too small. Without careful consideration of the implications for curriculum, implementing a MT-YRS calendar may result in what we are calling ghettoization of specific student groups on separate tracks. For example, if all of the ESL classes were on one track and the college prep courses on another, ghettoization would be the likely result. As we have seen in Stephen Lewis, where the school adheres to a middle school philosophy, this is not as likely an occurrence.

In the following lists, we focus on the specific advantages and disadvantages of YRE schedules for secondary schools. These are in addition to the items included in Chapters 1 and 2. These lists do not stand alone but should be read as supplements to the lists in the previous chapters.

Disadvantages of YRS at the Secondary Level

Some additional disadvantages are:

- extra work is made for secretaries and support personnel to track student courses and statistics
- students may have to participate in sports while off-track

- students may take "unfair" advantage of opportunities for remediation (by slacking off during the regular term)
- teachers choosing to teach regularly at intersession may experience burnout

Benefits of YRS for Secondary Schools

Some additional advantages are:

- increased chances for remediation
- opportunities for acceleration
- enrichment opportunities not usually offered in secondary school
- decrease in dropout rate
- increase in graduation courses completed
- increase in graduation rate
- flexibility for students
- facilitates student jobs
- benefits of participating in sports (and other extracurricular activities) while off-track
- increased learning opportunities for students
- increased opportunities for teacher employment during intersession
- students can accelerate graduation
- opportunities for work-release programs in intersession
- professional development opportunities for teachers (visiting other programs)
- better college preparation opportunities (students may take more classes)

CONCLUDING COMMENT

We have noted that, despite the obvious advantages, year-round schooling in secondary schools is relatively rare. One reason, we have suggested, is that scheduling in a secondary school already tends to be more complex than in an elementary school, and year-round calendars, particularly multi-track models, only exacerbate the situation. Second, large secondary schools, with their departmental organization, do not provide many opportunities for the development of a shared vision for change (although it is certainly possible to overcome this perceived deficit). Because teachers in secondary schools generally enjoy more autonomy and individual discretion than many elementary school teachers, coming together in a collaborative change initiative may seem somewhat foreign to the culture of many secondary school teachers.

A third reason for the limited use of year-round schedules at the secondary level may be misconceptions about the ability of students to engage in employment and to participate in sports, band, and other school-related activities when they are on a rotating schedule. Many of the students, educators, and parents with whom we spoke have dispelled these myths. Most said that a year-round schedule facilitates rather than inhibits their participation in co-curricular activities and employment beyond school.

We have not analyzed the financial implications of offering year-round schooling at the secondary level, however, one issue frequently raised is the funding of intersession programs. Many districts have chosen to reallocate funding normally assigned to summer school to intersession programs. In other situations, intersession is offered on a user-pay basis, as is summer school in the same jurisdiction. In still others, students are provided with free access to a course the first time but required to pay if they need to re-enroll to complete their credit.

In an era when high schools may need to increase the flexibility of their offerings to help students deal with the pressures of an increasingly complex society, we are surprised that year-round schooling still seems to be so rare. Single-track secondary school models, in particular, offer to students increased flexibility, personal choice, and extended learning opportunities, in concert with the opportunity to participate in a wide range of extracurricular and enrichment activities or to regroup or get back on-track as necessary. Intersession may present courses in bites that are easier for students to digest, may offer special interest classes that attract and maintain student interest, or enhance college readiness and standing. We envisage opportunities for students to engage in tutorials for college entry exams during intersession, for intensive ESL programs, conflict resolution, or enhanced work-study opportunities. As one of the teachers in our study stated, the possibilities are limited only by one's imagination. We believe the potential of year-round schooling at the secondary level remains largely untapped.

SECTION II:

RESEARCH AND PERSPECTIVES

Representatives from schools, districts, and parent committees wanting to explore calendar changes are frequently surprised how difficult it is to discover accurate, unbiased, and data-based information about year-round schooling. This section presents a research overview that is intended to help those examining the impact of the YR calendar. In the successive chapters we discuss what can be learned from the literature as well as from our own international, longitudinal research. In particular, we present data from students, parents, teachers, and administrators concerning their first-hand experiences with year-round schooling.

ASSESSING THE LITERATURE

The available published information on year-round schooling is extensive and uneven. We have tried to offer some guidance for those wanting to turn to the primary sources. Although we have excluded much of the literature that has an obvious and unsupported bias of some sort, some has been included to demonstrate how data are sometimes poorly used and how they should be interpreted with caution. When we refer to *bias*, we do not mean to imply that we believe the researcher's voice or position can, or should, ever be totally absent from the research. Indeed, every study is to some extent a reflection of the researcher's predispositions and assumptions. But *researcher bias* may sometimes lead to a failure to identify the characteristics of groups being studied or to describe methods of data collection or analysis.

Researcher bias appears in various ways in the YRS literature. Some reports or articles are clearly written to try to prevent the implementation of year-round schooling; others suggest, without providing supporting arguments, that it is the best thing since sliced bread. Studies sometimes report on newspaper headlines or articles that highlight the choice made by a given school or district to implement, or discontinue, year-round schooling. We have considered these statements biased sources of information unless supporting explanations were also included. Reliable research has internal consistency or validity, does not rely heavily on unsupported opinions, gives as complete a picture as possible, and is accomplished within appropriate timelines and clearly delineated methodology.

Much research about the impact of YRS has been conducted "in house," by sponsoring districts, during the first year of implementation; however, the first year may not be the best time to conduct an assessment. Experts on educational change recognize that change is generally accompanied by what they call an *implementation dip*. When a tennis player tries to change her grip on the racket, there is a period during which she appears to be a less skillful player than she was previously; so it is with educational change. Only after the tennis player has become used to the new grip can she determine whether it has, indeed, improved her game. As teachers, administrators, parents, and students experience a new concept, there is a time of getting acquainted and becoming comfortable with the innovation. Only after this period has passed can the impact of the change on student performance be appropriately assessed.

Although some local evaluation is valid, in other cases, some of the questions used are ill constructed and the findings dubious. For example, the question, "How much better do you like school this year [on a year-round schedule] than last year?" will not generate any meaningful data. It will be unclear how much the respondent liked school the previous year or to what one might really attribute any reported change (new teacher, change in family situation, etc.). Perhaps most importantly, asking how much better a respondent likes something is inherently biased because it presupposes that the respondent does prefer the innovation. Here, the only question being asked is one of degree. Such interpretations, while perhaps useful for supporting local agendas, do not really add to sound research-based knowledge about year-round schooling.

In the following chapters, we attempt to present the literature in a helpful manner, to assist those wanting to make decisions one way or another about year-round schooling for their specific contexts. To present as complete a picture as possible, we use the literature as a background for the empirical data from our studies.

INTRODUCING OUR DATA

In this section, we offer some data based analyses of the impact of year-round schooling on a number of participant groups. The discussion in each chapter extends the overview of what other researchers have described in the literature and summarizes what we have identified as key issues and findings reported by students, parents, teachers, and administrators.

Most of the student data are drawn from our six-year longitudinal study conducted in Delphi[1] district, a large, metropolitan district in Utah, a state with one of the highest per capita numbers of students in year-round schooling. The district serves more than 58,000 students in seven high schools, 13 junior high schools, seven alternative programs, and 48 elementary schools. Of the 48 elementary schools, 34 follow the traditional-calendar school (TCS) year, 12 use a multi-track year-round calendar, and two schools, which opened in August 1995, began with a single-track year-round calendar and changed to a multi-track calendar in the fall of 1996. The 12 year-round schools, some of which have been operating on a MT-YRS schedule since 1989, represent 25% of the elementary schools and approximately 36% of the elementary students. They are relatively large, housing between 410 and 1242 students each. The district's traditional-calendar schools are also quite large, with populations between 366 and 854 students. Our data include surveys conducted with more than 1000 fifth graders as well as longitudinal standardized test data that includes the same group of students.

---

[1]We remind you that all names of districts, schools, and individuals from our research are pseudonyms.

Data from parents are also drawn from this Utah district, where we conducted surveys in eight schools, three traditional-calendar, three multi-track, and the two new single-track schools. In all, more than 650 parents responded to our surveys.

In addition, we have held meetings, conducted observations, and engaged in extensive interviews in 17 school districts from British Columbia to Florida and from Ontario to California. More than 48 school-based administrators, 19 district representatives, and more than 100 teachers from five states and four Canadian provinces have been interviewed or surveyed. We are convinced that the size and extent of our database provide a credible basis for the discussions that follow.

CONCLUSION

In Chapter 4 we focus our attention on the impact of year-round schooling on students, in terms of academic and nonacademic issues. Chapter 5 provides an overview of parental perceptions and experiences with year-round calendars. In Chapter 6, we describe the experiences of teachers and their perceptions of the impact of the YRS calendar on their personal and professional lives and on the education of their students. In Chapter 7, we turn to an examination of the challenges that YR calendars offer administrators and describe their insights concerning the potential benefits and disadvantages. We also examine some issues that affect the quality and success of the implementation of YR schedules. We hope that you will find these next four chapters, in which we combine relevant literature with our own findings and experiences, useful and thought provoking.

CHAPTER 4:

THE IMPACT OF YEAR-ROUND SCHOOLING
ON STUDENTS

The only reason anyone in this district is considering year-round schooling is to save money. They say that some studies show they can even save money and have no impact on the students. "No difference!" That's not good enough for me and it certainly isn't good enough for our kids! (Parent)

*****

Any educational reform initiative is accompanied by concern about its effects on student learning. Assessing student achievement, either academic or nonacademic outcomes, is a complex issue, and single measures based on standardized tests or self-assessment inventories cannot provide more than small pieces of the puzzle. This does not mean, of course, that those types of evaluation should be disregarded, but that the total picture needs to be constructed from a variety of sources and studies. Appraising these effects is complicated by a number of factors, including the possible political agendas of proponents and opponents, researcher and educator bias, perceptions of the general public, and the need for immediate feedback—sometimes prior to the next election.

The first part of this chapter deals with student academic achievement as it is described in the research literature and then through our findings in Delphi District. In the second part of the chapter, we discuss the relationship between year-round school calendars and some of the most commonly identified student nonacademic outcomes, such as enjoyment of school, student employment opportunities, and dropout rates.

THE LITERATURE RELATED TO STUDENT ACADEMIC ACHIEVEMENT

Most of the studies conducted during the past three decades present a fairly confusing picture about the impact of year-round schooling on student achievement. In part, this has been due to the preponderance of writing that takes a position for, or against, a calendar change. In addition, methodological difficulties have accounted for much of the confusion. In the research, there is often little differentiation between single-track and multi-track year-round schooling. Likewise, many articles fail to indicate how they have assessed success or failure, whether the findings are statistically significant or whether they represent slight gains or losses that may be attributed to chance. For example, one review of YRS research found that only four of 17 reported studies had results that were statistically significant, although in each case the authors had drawn conclusions about the success of the year-round calendar.

The need for schools and districts to quickly evaluate the success of a new year-round calendar has led to many studies being undertaken within the first year of implementation. These data are unreliable measures of long-term effects. On occasion, there has been a tendency for a noticeable increase in academic performance during the first year, but within a couple of years, there has been a leveling off slightly below the initial peak. Sometimes, as Winters (1995) found in National City, California, the first-year results exhibit a decline and then subsequently increase and level off. The literature reinforces common wisdom that assessment and evaluation of new programs cannot be conducted reliably within the first year of a project.

Many studies have found that year-round schooling is associated with improvements in student academic achievement (Baker, 1990; Bradford, 1993; Grotjohn & Banks, 1993; Kneese, 1996; Los Angeles Unified School District, 1983; Mutchler, 1993; Peltier, 1991; Perry, 1991; Winters, 1995). Other careful reviews of the literature (Goren & Carriedo, 1986; Hazelton et al, 1992; Merino, 1983; Zykowski et al., 1991) have identified research that reports either a slight gain or, at minimum, no difference when the academic achievement of students in traditional and year-round schools was compared. Although the finding of "no difference" has frequently been used as an argument against implementing YRS, Shields and LaRocque

(1997) posited that a finding of "no difference" in student achievement should be interpreted in a relatively positive light, because it demonstrates that it is possible for structural change, increased facility use, and cost benefits to occur without negative consequences to important student outcomes.

There is compelling evidence that the positive effects of YRS are enhanced for students in at-risk groups (Atwood, 1983; Capps & Cox, 1991; Gandara & Fish, 1994; Perry, 1991; Serifs, 1990). One apparent exception frequently cited in the literature is the study by Quinlan and associates (1987). They found that student achievement in multi-track year-round schools in the large, urban community studied was lower than in other schools; however, they added that this was neither unexpected nor attributable to YRS, but likely due to a number of other factors inherent in the setting.

A few other studies show a mixed impact on student achievement. Harlan (1973) found that students with IQs below 100 were negatively affected by the YR calendar. A San Diego study conducted in 1994 (Fass-Holmes & Gates) found that YRS had a negative impact on its experimental middle school, but that it had a positive impact on the achievement of its elementary single-track schools.

Some researchers have attempted to determine whether the impact of YRS calendars varies based on gender or race. In one Ohio study, YRS was found to have a positive overall impact, most notably on male students. However, Cooper and associates (1996) found no differences in summer learning loss based on gender. Their study also supported the finding of Heyns (1987) that there were no differences by race when socioeconomic status (SES) was taken into consideration. Indeed, students in lower socioeconomic levels were those most negatively affected by learning loss over the long traditional summer vacation (*Learning* . . . , 1978). Thus, at-risk students appear to reap the greatest benefits from a modified school year calendar that offers the possibility of intersession or an increased number of school days.

Most of the studies previously cited suggest that where gains in achievement have been found, the underlying reasons have not yet been well explored. Nevertheless, the literature identifies three possible explanations.

The first theory is that many schools that change their calendar also focus on changing some of their curricular materials and instructional practices (Goren & Carriedo, 1986; Hough et al, 1990; White, 1992). In our own studies of the impact of year-round schooling, we have frequently found that YRS can provide the impetus for instructional change. We concur with the literature that suggests that achievement gains may be attributable, in part, to concomitant changes in programs and instructional practices that may have been stimulated by a change in school calendar.

The second hypothesis has to do with theories and research concerning remembering or forgetting. Some (Allinder et al., 1992; Capps & Cox, 1991) assert that the issue of forgetting and retaining is complex and involves more than simply time. Others relate retention to family socio-economic status. A report by the New York State Board of Regents in 1978 (*Learning, . . .*) found differential learning for advantaged and disadvantaged students. Advantaged students typically make 15 months worth of academic gains during the school year and experience additional growth in the summer, for a total of approximately 16 month's growth each year. In contrast, disadvantaged students make roughly 12 months worth of academic gains during the school year, then lose three to four month's worth during the summer, for a net gain of seven to eight months. Entwistle and Alexander conducted studies that involved both white and African-American students. They found that children from low SES families (1992) and children of less educated parents (1994) lost "in *absolute* achievement over the summer months in math and reading, respectively, while high SES students of both races actually gained in absolute achievement" (cited in Jamar, 1994, p. 6–7, italics in original).

Finally, the literature emphasizes that where there are gains, the improvement may be due to student attendance at intersession, which in essence results in an extended school year. Several examples of intersession programming were cited in the first few chapters of this book. In Jefferson County, Colorado, high school students in a multi-track school were permitted to attend an additional academic session during one vacation period (White, 1988). In Tennessee, an experiment in which students were offered a voluntary fourth (summer) quarter was suspended after its second year due to under-utilization (Banta, 1978), although a similar plan has been highly successful in Buena Vista County, Virginia, where over a 20 year period, student attendance in the summer quarter ranged from 41-67%, with an average of slightly over 50%

(Bradford, 1996). In each case, intersession offered the opportunity for students to engage in remediation, enrichment, or acceleration. Other reports on student achievement from secondary schools tend to be relatively inconclusive regarding test scores but emphasize that a YR calendar was frequently accompanied by increased attendance and lower dropout rates (especially in the senior year).

Taken together, the literature suggests that YRS has, at worst, no impact on student academic performance and, at best, may be associated with gains. This seems particularly true for students in "at-risk" groups. Although some of the gains are not particularly meaningful, others are statistically significant.

STUDENT ACADEMIC ACHIEVEMENT IN DELPHI SCHOOL DISTRICT

We had the unique opportunity to test some of the research findings concerning student academic performance by examining student results on a state-mandated standardized test over a six-year period. Although we recognize that standardized testing constitutes only a small part of the necessary evidence of student learning, the data do provide useful information for understanding trends related to student achievement.

Our study was conducted in a large urban district in Utah where we compared the performance of all students from Delphi District's elementary traditional-calendar schools with the performance of all students from its schools using a multi-track year-round calendar. We analyzed the academic achievement of fifth grade students using the data that the school district made available to us from the Statewide Testing Program. Data from the scores on the norm-referenced tests were analyzed in two ways.

First, consistent with the approach taken elsewhere (Alkin, 1983; Merino, 1983; Mutchler, 1993, Peltier, 1991), we compared the mean fifth grade scores of all the traditional-calendar schools with those of the multi-track schools on the total battery and subtests of the norm-referenced Stanford Achievement Test. Our first analysis produced relatively similar (and inconclusive) findings. A t-test for independent samples with unequal groups identified only one statistically significant difference between the two types of schools. In 1994, reading scores were found to be significantly higher in multi-track schools than in traditional-calendar schools (t = 2.24; p = .032; sig < .05). All other differences in all years were found to be non-significant, although the mean scores for the year-round schedule were slightly higher than for traditional schools. In other words, the 1994 difference in the reading scores may reasonably be attributed to a difference in school calendar, whereas all non-significant differences in this and other years may be attributed to chance.

Our second analysis provided the most conclusive results. We compared all of the scores achieved in the six-year period from 1990 to 1996 with the predicted achievement bands for each school as established by the Utah State Office of Education. Each year, to recognize that there are important differences among the respective student bodies in a district, the State Office of Education makes available to schools an annually established predicted range of achievement for each of the tests and subtests required by the State-wide Testing Program. This predicted range of achievement is based on a formula that takes into consideration factors relevant to socio-economic status. Thus, even as school demographics change, a school can readily assess the performance of its students for a given year relative to what might reasonably be expected in light of its particular population and demographics. In addition, schools can identify their own performance trends in terms of how well they attained, exceeded, or fell below, scores within the range expected for them over time.

For schools with each type of calendar, we identified the percentage of scores that fell within, above, or below their predicted range, compared to all of the possible scores for the calendar type. Over the six years, 21% of the 1200 scores from the district's traditional calendar schools fell below their predicted range, whereas only 4% of the 330 scores from multi-track year-round schools fell below the range of achievement predicted for their school.[1]

The data from our study supported the findings from other studies in that we also found that YRS were associated with higher levels of student achievement (Baker, 1990; Bradford, 1993; Los Angeles Unified School District, 1983; Mutchler, 1993; Peltier, 1991; Perry, 1991). The difference of 17% in the percentage of scores within or above the predicted range between 1990 and 1996 is indicative of

[1]For a more complete discussion of these findings, see Shields and Oberg (1999).

a substantive positive difference in achievement for the MT-YRS in Delphi District.

YRS AND NON-ACADEMIC OUTCOMES

The term *student nonacademic outcomes* is so broad that it covers a myriad of aspects of student school life. Here, we offer an overview of some of the salient issues based on our experience, surveys, interviews, and questionnaires, and on the YRS literature. Although most of our student data come from the elementary school surveys conducted in Delphi District, we supplement our data for secondary schools with information gleaned from student interviews conducted elsewhere. In this section, we attempt to respond to a number of frequently asked questions and concerns about YRS.

Student Attitudes

Most parents, teachers, and administrators with experience with YRS report that students have had generally positive feelings about the year-round calendar; students themselves generally agree (Alkin, 1983; Baker, 1990; Barrett et al., 1992; Christie, 1989; Gandara, 1992; Hazelton et al., 1992; LAUSD, 1983; Perry, 1991; Zykowski et al., 1991). Although some of these researchers specifically noted that students in YRS enjoy school more than those in traditional schools, this was not supported by our own student survey data. For us, students on traditional and YR calendars reported no difference in their enjoyment of school on surveys of nonacademic student outcomes.

In our first elementary school study (Shields & Oberg, 1995), we compared the responses of 135 students from traditional schools and 174 students from multi-track year-round schools. We found that for students in both types of school, education was equally and highly important. They reported having missed the same average number of days of school, the same level of anticipation about returning to school after a school break, and believed they retained approximately the same amount of what they had previously learned. Likewise, we found no significant or substantive differences in the amount of homework done or in the amount of individual help students received from their teachers. Students on both school calendars also indicated, not surprisingly, most of their friends were from the same school.

Extracurricular

When a district begins to consider a move to a year-round calendar, questions inevitably arise concerning the potential impact on extracurricular activities. In general, students in year-round schools reported they were able to maintain or improve their involvement in extracurricular activities. Most schools that changed to a YR calendar indicated that the number of activities offered did not decrease. In fact, sometimes we found that with the inception of intersession, schools introduced more opportunities for student involvement in clubs and other types of activities. Elementary students in multi-track schools were frequently able to return to school, even when off-track, to participate in extracurricular activities, such as band, choral performances, or clubs.

For secondary students, the situation was somewhat more complex. Sometimes coaches were nervous that students who were off-track would not attend practices or competitions during their vacation time. However, students from YRS reported that the opposite tended to be the case. For example, some said it was helpful, while off-track, to be able to compete in a basketball tournament without also having to worry about completing homework.

In general, student comments from our data supported the findings of White (1988) and Zykowski and associates (1991) who found that year-round school facilitates involvement in extracurricular activities.

Employment

Employment is, of course, primarily a concern at the high school level. Students frequently informed us that, contrary to some fears, year-round schooling had a positive impact on their employment opportunities. Students in single-track secondary schools suggested that it was easy to request additional hours from an employer during school breaks, especially as most of their student co-workers were still in school. For those who were able to have the month of

December off, YRS enabled full-time employment for the pre-Christmas period and a return to school following the break. Regularly scheduled three-week breaks also facilitated co-op and work-study programs, which, in turn, led to more permanent employment.

Our data are consistent with the findings of Howell (1988). That not all students seek employment at the same time, coupled with the fact that students have breaks in which work does not interfere with either academic or extracurricular activities, seems positive.

Motivation and Burnout

We found, as have others (Hazelton et al., 1992; Zykowski et al., 1991), that students in YRS seemed more ready to learn and to maintain their motivation throughout the year than their peers in traditional schools. Most children indicated that the summer vacation associated with the traditional calendar became long and often boring; many reported they were ready to return to school earlier. The three-week breaks distributed throughout the school year appeared to be almost ideal for a reprieve from the routine of schooling. Teachers and parents, as well as students, reported that just as motivation was dwindling, school breaks occurred; likewise, everyone seemed ready to return following the breaks.

Some secondary students found sustaining momentum for academics for a whole semester or school year was difficult. Breaking the term into smaller chunks and assigning quarter credits along with intersession support seemed to help them to maintain momentum and to achieve academic success.

School Attendance and Dropouts

There is a consensus in the literature that YRS reduces the student dropout rate, facilitates retention in school, and increases student attendance (Baker, 1990; Bradford, 1993; Brekke, 1983: LAUSD, 1983; White, 1987; White, 1988). This finding seems to relate to the previous notions that higher and more sustained levels of motivation, increased school success, and sustained involvement in extracurricular activities may be associated with better attendance and completion rates. We have also found that if a student has missed an extended period of time due to family circumstances or personal illness, sometimes he or she is permitted to attend a class on a different track during a break. The opportunity to spend time during the break to catch up may facilitate moving ahead with peers.

The benefits of a MT calendar may be increased in high schools where students sometimes become discouraged and drop out of school or where loss of credits sometimes delays graduation or prevents entry into subsequent programs. When intersession offers the opportunity for a student who has failed a class to retake it and not repeat a whole year, the benefits are considerable.

Thus, the increased opportunities offered by both ST and MT-YRS for enrichment, for catch-up, and for remediation offered by the more regular pattern of schooling and vacation, and sometimes enhanced by intersession programs, seems to have an indisputably positive effect on student attendance and course completion.

Decrease in Vandalism and Student Delinquency

Many year-round schools reported a decreased incidence of student vandalism and their communities noted a concomitant decrease in juvenile crime (Ballinger, 1987; Brekke, 1983; Hazelton et al., 1992; Merino, 1983). The respondents to our surveys and interviews reported similar benefits. Some hypothesized that decreased vandalism might be associated with increased use of school facilities over a longer portion of the school year. Others suggested that decreased juvenile crime might be attributed, in part, to reduced student boredom and to smaller numbers of students not in school at any one time. One reported difficulty was that it is often hard for community and business representatives to know which students should be in school and which are legitimately on breaks at any given time. A solution to this potential truancy problem, implemented by some MT-YRS, has been to include students' scheduled vacation times on the backs of their ID cards.

Participation in Community Activities

We found no evidence that students in YRS participated in more community activities than their counterparts in traditional schools;

neither was there evidence that their participation was curtailed, despite fears expressed by some community groups and associations. Zykowski and associates (1991) stated that summer recreation leagues and camps reported no adverse effects from YRS. In other areas, some community service groups made changes or modified their programs or delivery schedules because of the implementation of year-round schooling. For example, some YWCAs began to offer swimming lessons in three-week blocks throughout the year to coincide with the YRS breaks. Most community groups seemed to have willingly accommodated to changes in the school calendar. As one representative stated, "We're here to serve the public." Perhaps because of the need for increased communication and consultation with the public over the implementation of a modified school calendar, personnel from YRS also indicated that they had better contacts with social services, law enforcement, and other community groups than they had had previously. Again, this is consistent with other reported research (Hazelton et al., 1992).

Increased Retention and Learning Opportunities

One of the central arguments advanced by proponents of YRS is that it promotes an increase in student learning. Alcorn (1991) associated the shorter summer vacation of YRS with less learning loss than experienced by students in traditional-calendar schools. Others identified increased retention with the more frequent, but shorter, breaks. Increased learning was also related to less time spent by teachers on review activities and more academic learning time for students (Ballinger, 1987, 1988; Ballinger et al., 1987; O'Neil & Adamson, 1993; Weaver, 1992). The possibility of attending intersession also provided the students with opportunities for more sustained learning and less forgetting than the traditional school year. The prospects offered by enrichment activities, additional course options, and creative instructional strategies significantly enhance the potential of YRS to increase learning. The research indicates that students in YRS tend to participate in additional educational programs offered between tracks or sessions more often than students in traditional-calendar schools participated in comparable summer programs (Bradford, 1993).

CONCLUSION

In this chapter, we have presented both an overview of the literature and some information drawn from our own research to provide a general sense of the impact of year-round schooling on students. We have found that there is little or no negative impact on
either academic or nonacademic outcomes. On the contrary, there
is increasing evidence that many students benefit academically
when a school changes to a year-round calendar. Moreover, the
benefits accrue to at-risk students and those who are not, to those
who have the opportunity to attend intersession and to those who
do not, to those who are in single-track as well as multi-track
schools, and to elementary as well as secondary students. Three
main reasons were advanced for the benefits: decreased learning
loss over a shorter summer vacation, increased opportunities for
remediation or enrichment through intersession, and changes in
school programs and pedagogical approaches related to, but not
necessarily caused by, the change to a year-round calendar.

Our examination and discussion of various nonacademic issues
suggests that there are often benefits of the year-round calendar for
students, schools, and communities related to better opportunities
for employment, increased motivation for learning, reduced dropout rates, and decreased vandalism. It is not wise, however, to
promise these benefits to any specific community without a careful examination of how year-round schooling might be implemented in that unique context. For example, although we conclude,
based on our understanding of the research, that YRS positively
benefits at-risk students in the inner-city, contextual factors related
to the discrete population, socio-political matters, and the
community's unique problems and needs may have a substantial
impact on these findings.

In Chapter 2, we presented a portrait of Jerico Elementary School
in which we outlined a number of additional programs that were
implemented within the framework of YRS. A claim that YRS
moved the school off of Florida's critically low list, without a consideration of the attendant program changes and implementation
strategies would be inappropriate. In Chapter 3, we described some
of the organizational features that accompanied the move to a
single-track schedule for Persephone High School. Again, a blan-
ket claim that single-track YRS is beneficial at the high school level

without knowing how it was implemented in this, or any other context, would be an inadequate interpretation and use of the research.

We are aware that the previous overview presents an optimistic perspective on the academic and nonacademic benefits of YRS. This is, in fact, consistent with most of the available research. The body of research concerning the impact of year-round schooling on student achievement and on other factors related to student life is increasingly positive. However, the more we build up a positive picture of the effects of year-round schooling, the more we have also become aware that the calendar change usually acts as a catalyst for other types of pedagogical change. For YRS to be successful in terms of its impact on students, educators need to carefully consider how to maximize its benefits for the local context.

CHAPTER 5:

THE IMPACT OF YEAR-ROUND SCHOOLING

ON PARENTS

My child has been in traditional, single-track, and multi-track schools and none of those seem to really matter. If she has a good teacher, it is a positive experience. The only thing that seems to make a difference is the teacher—that's what really matters. (Parent)

*****

We get all kinds of people at these meetings. Some parents are very supportive. Then there are groups like PAM—Parents Against Multi-tracking—that make things really difficult. Whenever district representatives try to correct their misperceptions, they accuse us of being advocates, trying to ram YRS down their throats. In fact, there's a faction I like to call CAVE—Citizens Against Virtually Everything. (Superintendent)

*****

There is no doubt that very few issues stir up public emotions like a proposed change to the education system. In part, this is because of a general tendency to be wary of change. Where public schooling is concerned, this is compounded by the fact that most parents have had experience with formal education and consider themselves to be knowledgeable and even to have some kind of expertise—as long as schooling is presented "the way it used to be." In fact, the adage, "If it was good enough for me, it's good enough for my children" is frequently heard when educational change is proposed.

Among recent educational changes that cause some confusion among parents and educators alike, is a movement towards increased empowerment of parents and parent councils. Regardless of the lack of clarity surrounding the role of parents in public education, the value of attaining their support for a proposed educational innovation likely cannot be overstated. In fact, one expert asserted that "one of the essential conditions for the success and implementation of year-round schooling must be the degree to which parents and the community at large are favorably disposed to a change in the traditional schedule" (Merino, 1983, p. 303). This position is supported by our research in many jurisdictions both in the United States and in Canada.

For example, in 1994, faced with rapidly escalating capital costs due to increased enrollment, the Ministry of Education of British Columbia offered funds to school districts to study the possible implementation of year-round schooling. Following the year of study and consultation, none of the districts decided to proceed with any model of year-round schooling. Overwhelmingly negative perceptions on the part of parent groups influenced the decision of each district. This is reminiscent of a group in Seneca Valley, Pennsylvania, the Citizens Against Year-Round Education, reported by Rasberry (1994) to have rejoiced when the district curtailed its study of the calendar change.

Consultation with parent groups is generally an important part of a district's preliminary investigation into the feasibility of year-round schooling (YRS). However, it is particularly important to recognize that there may be a disparity between the concerns raised by parents who have never experienced YRS—concerns often fueled by rumor, special interest groups, or the media—and the responses and perceptions of parents who have had firsthand experience with a new calendar.

In this chapter,[1] we identify and examine several issues generally raised by parents concerning the impact of YRS on the child, the family, the school, and the community. The basis for this report is our study of parents in Delphi District. There, we were able to compare the degree of parental support or satisfaction for year-round schools with the responses of parents with children in traditional calendar schools. This is a particularly useful group of

[1]We are indebted to the *Journal of Educational Administration and Foundations* for permitting us to present this simplified version of an earlier article. For a more detailed report of this research, see Shields and Oberg (1997).

respondents because of their relatively long experience with, and knowledge of, year-round schooling. Since 1989, when the district first introduced multi-track year-round schooling, the number of schools and students has gradually increased. By 1995 and 1996 when our data were collected, approximately 36% of its elementary school children were enrolled in 12 year-round schools (representing 25% of the total number of schools).

This chapter reports the responses of more than 650 parents in Delphi School District. Approximately 200 of them had children in traditional-calendar schools, 250 in multi-track year-round schools, and more than 200 had children in ST schools that changed to MT calendars during our study. For the most part, there were no differences between the responses of parents with children in single-track or multi-track schools. Where differences existed we describe them separately. Before presenting our own findings, we describe some other published studies dealing with parental attitudes to YRS.

WHAT RESEARCH SAYS ABOUT PARENTAL PERCEPTIONS

One of the areas most frequently studied and reported in the year-round school literature is the topic of parental perceptions and support for the YR calendar. Although the body of literature is mixed in terms of methodological soundness and subsequent findings, the quantity itself suggests the importance generally attributed to the topic.

In 1983, Merino, in one of the most cited studies of year-round schooling, identified as part of her review of the literature, six studies that had been conducted between 1974 and 1980 of parents' attitudes toward year-round education. Perhaps not surprisingly, she found that people with no experience of year-round schooling were usually negatively disposed toward it, whereas those with experience tended to favor it. Equally predictable were the results of a study conducted by Sardo-Brown and Rooney (1992), in which 236 households of students enrolled in the first year of a pilot project were surveyed, only 10% of respondents wanted to adopt a year-round school calendar on a permanent basis.

Misinformation concerning the implementation of year-round schooling is abundant. For example, Rasberry (1994) cited com-

ments from newspaper reports from 26 different states and concluded "many find [year-round school] is not the answer" (p. 10).
Many of the citations referred to perceptions prior to implementation: "The Trumball school district decided not to pilot a year-round
program, to the relief of concerned parents" (p. 11); "five . . . schools
dropped the idea because of a lack of community support; [. . .] significant opposition from parents and cost defeated YRS in four communities" (p. 12); and "angry parents and students overwhelmingly
refused to accept a radical change in the school year" (p. 13). Other
items, also drawn from news articles, although perhaps accurate in
themselves, tended to be misleading. Rasberry stated that "Silver
Mesa Elementary in the Jordan School District [Utah] returned to
the traditional calendar, ending a year of intense community controversy" (p. 17). She added, "A decline in the number of students
at the school made the program no longer feasible" (p. 17). While
this was true, the implication is misleading unless one also knows
that 24 of the district's 47 elementary schools continued to operate
successfully on a multi-track year-round schedule.

Baker (1990) reviewed 10 studies conducted during the 1980s and
found, in each, quite positive parental perceptions. In Tacoma,
Washington, "Seventy percent of parents with year-round experience felt that educational quality was the same as in traditional
schools" (p. 18). In Los Angeles, California, "most parents believed
that their child's attitude about school, and achievement, behavior,
homework, and attendance were better" (p. 19). In 1985, in Cherry
Creek, Colorado, "after three years of the year-round calendar, parents voted to keep it" (p. 20). In her own study of parents of children in a pilot program in Conroe Independent School District,
Baker concluded by stating that her "nul hypothesis" was accepted
in that "there [was] no significant difference in parental satisfaction
with year-round and traditional school calendars" (p. 87).

LEARNING FROM PARENTS IN DELPHI DISTRICT

The parents in our study provided firsthand information about the
impact of YRS. Reviewing the responses from parents in Delphi
District, we found it interesting, and perhaps worthy of note, that
parents with children in YRS wrote more extensively and expressed
themselves with more emotion (both for and against the YRS

calendar) than parents of children in traditional-calendar schools. This difference is reflected in the comments in the following section as we examine how parents believed the calendar had affected students, families, the school itself, and the communities within which the schools were situated.

Impact on Students

Most parents of students from year-round schools were positive about their local version of the 45-15 schedule. Their perception was that the three-week breaks resulted in considerably less boredom during vacation time, better retention of learned material, and less stress and burnout for students. Comments like the following were fairly typical of these parents: "My children enjoy the breaks. . . . They do not get as bored as with traditional school. The experience for our children has been excellent. I don't want it any other way!" "My child learns more . . . she forgets less between school years and she is less likely to get extremely bored with school because of the three-week breaks." One parent commented that the calendar helped to instill family values:

> I like the breaks to have my kids get back to being "family-centered" instead of so "friend-centered." Some friends they rub shoulders with daily at school aren't the best influences. Some "attitudes" they get exposed to start to dissolve after a couple of days of being home full-time.

Among the benefits identified by the parents of children in schools with traditional calendars was the perception that it was easier to participate in both family and community activities. This was particularly true if families also had other children on different calendars in junior or senior high school. In addition, some parents believed that the traditional school-year organization helped their children by providing a more consistent routine. Other perceived benefits included time at home during the summer to "learn and experience other aspects of life and fun," to have a "chance to do 'home school' and focus on individual needs and interests." One parent identified the need to "catch up on being a child. It seems that there is more competition and children are pushed more to learn faster these days. Sometimes we forget the benefits of relaxation and the free, imaginative playtime [that] summers allow." Another parent expressed it this way: "traditional is safe—we've never had anything else: everything is standard—long summer vacation, regular holiday breaks, etc."

Of course, neither group of parents thought its schedule was perfect. Parents from traditional-calendar schools frequently indicated that they believed a three-month break to be too long and identified student boredom, interruption of learning, less retention of material learned, and the need for more reviewing following the summer as the primary disadvantages. "I feel they lose a lot during the summer and the schools have to spend too much time reviewing and catching up," or "he gets bored and even though we try to keep him busy, he has to relearn each year." One observed, "It is a long school year with few breaks. But I survived the same schedule as a child, . . . maybe year-round would help."

Parents of children from year-round schools also talked about school breaks. Some of them felt that learning was interrupted by the three-week breaks and that the year-round schedule interrupted student routines: "We don't do well on stopping and starting schedules. Once we get into a routine we do great but beginning and ending takes a while to shift gears. As a result, homework, sleep, routine, etc. suffer each time there is a break." Parents of children in year-round schools were also concerned that sometimes their children were home alone while the rest of the family was involved with school or work, and sometimes the elementary year-round students were at school when older siblings were at home on break.

The disadvantages most frequently identified by parents who had children in YR schools related to the fact that friends and other family members were sometimes on different tracks or schedules, making interaction more difficult. "Friends and neighbors are not always off-track and able to play or see each other at the same time." One parent wrote at length about how difficult it had been to move into a new community and to get to know the children from the neighborhood when they were on four different tracks. She commented, "I feel absolutely no unity as a community and my children have suffered greatly because of it."

Some parents from each group clearly would have preferred a different calendar. Some patrons of YRS indicated that a traditional schedule would prevent them from having to take their child out of school for family reunions and activities. A few parents of traditional-school children responded that they would prefer to have their children on year-round schedules: "Traditional has been great but I wouldn't hesitate going to year-round for our benefit. It would give us time through the year together and I believe the children can retain better."

Each calendar had advantages and disadvantages for individual children, primarily related to the enjoyment of breaks and vacation periods and how they were perceived to help or hinder student learning. This also appeared to be true when the benefits or drawbacks to families were examined.

Impact on Families

Parents of children in traditional-calendar schools focused primarily on two issues: the benefits that accrue to families by having all of their children on the same schedule and the opportunities for families to enjoy summer activities and vacations together. "Since I have children in elementary, junior high, and high school, it is nice for all of us to be on the same schedule. We are able to spend quality time together as a family." Another representative comment was, "A non-traditional schedule would severely disrupt our family and would be a hardship to family work schedules, daycare, etc."

Parents of students on year-round calendars enjoyed having time off throughout the year to permit families to take advantage of different seasonal events. "We enjoy our 'off-track' time together—we use this time for family field trips—mini-vacation, etc." "[YRS] allows time during different parts of the year to take short vacations." Other perceived benefits were spreading "childcare expenses over the whole year" and having "more availability to give my child individual time to review school subjects and work on our relationship with each other." In fact, several parents noted that the year-round schedule permitted them to have "quality time" on a more regular basis with their children and indicated that they had asked for their children to be on different tracks. One parent elaborated this way, "It has been great for our family. There have been times that we have had our children on two different tracks to allow one-on-one time with Mom at home. I like the flexibility year-round offers us. We have tried all the tracks and have enjoyed the benefits of each."

Commenting on the disadvantages of their respective schedules for their family, parents of children from traditional schools tended to suggest that the school year and the summer breaks were too long. They were "unable to space vacations out" and were "more limited in family vacation choices." Several believed that the summer was too long and that their children forgot how to study. A small number felt that childcare was more difficult over the long summer period.

The disadvantages of YRS fell into three main categories: disruption to family routine and activities when children were in schools with different calendars, the difficulty of family activities in the summer, and problems finding childcare (several called it "a pain"). Often parent comments against the YR calendar were quite vehement: "The disruption! I have one in college, one in high school, one in junior high, and one in grade school. His schedule is by far the most difficult to work around, and we never seem to spend the time together that we used to. I hate it." Another agreed, "Vacations suck." Some went beyond describing the problem of arranging family activities to comment on their perceptions of the effect of the year-round calendar in more sociological terms. "Our children will resent one another for time off," declared one; "I think it is another way our society is breaking down the family," asserted another. However, not all perceived disadvantages were expressed as strongly. Some made statements like "it makes it a little difficult to go many places in the summer," or "it is inconvenient—we are dealing with it just fine, though."

It is apparent that, despite perceived strengths and educational advantages of year-round schools, when families have children on different schedules in different schools, the coordination and "juggling of family activities" become major problems for many families.

Impact on the School Itself

Parents of children in both types of schools identified numerous benefits of their respective calendars for the school itself, most concentrating either on the school as a physical entity or on the issue of teacher burnout. Here, one of the interesting features was that, although they had children on different schedules, parents' perceptions of advantages and disadvantages were fairly similar.

Parents indicated that not having their traditional-calendar school open in the summer eliminated costs associated with air-conditioning and hence saved money. At the same time, they believed that the long summer breaks permitted thorough cleaning and repairing, and reduced the "wear and tear" on the school. One commented, "The school is allowed to rest." Parents of children on year-round schedules also posited benefits related to school facilities. The school, they maintained, was less crowded, accommodated more students, was used more efficiently, had less wear and tear, and saved taxpayers money.

Parents of children on both traditional and year-round calendars each felt that their own calendar best provided teachers with needed breaks and helped to reduce burnout. In particular, the parents of children from YRS noted that smaller class size was associated with "less teacher stress," "better control of discipline problems," and "more individual attention." In addition, the schedule provided for more "interaction between teachers" and "a happier, more eager teacher and a more educated, eager student." Parents with children on a traditional-school calendar also mentioned benefits related directly to issues of learning and school climate. These included "continuity and security," a "feeling of unity," a "better group feeling," and the development of "togetherness as a school."

Parents of children in traditional-calendar schools noted the overcrowding of their buildings and the emptiness in the summer as the primary drawbacks. In addition, they mentioned that even though their school was not open as much in the summer, it did get hot when students were still in attendance and that it would benefit from air-conditioning. In fact, several parents were convinced that the additional money that seemed available to renovate or upgrade year-round schools was depriving traditional calendar schools of funds needed to upgrade their facilities. "It seems that schools who are on alternative schedules are given money for improvements, air conditioning, etc. It is very difficult to get money for a traditional school to make repairs, needed improvements. We all pay the same taxes—it doesn't seem fair to punish traditional schools."

Some parents of children in YRS were concerned about whether their school was adequately maintained and repaired without the long summer breaks. Others raised issues not related to the building, but rather to the overall educational climate of the school. These parents wondered if the interruptions to the school year and changing classes might cause extra stress or burnout for teachers. In addition, they noted that many of the school activities (assemblies, awards nights, field trips, etc.) had to be repeated to include all students and, even then, some students were not able to participate in every activity offered at the school. These parents were also concerned about the effect of year-round schooling on school unity. This concern was summed up by the parent who wrote, "I'm certain the school struggles with generating a spirit of cohesiveness and unity when 20% or so of the student body is always gone. School unity used to bond kids. What do they have now?"

Impact on Communities

Traditional-calendar patrons tended to agree that "community activities are still geared to traditional school, i.e., recreation programs, swimming lessons, etc." and observed that "when all the kids have the same vacation it is easier to plan community participation in after-hours sports" and other activities. Some parents of children in YRS reported that their communities had adapted. They stated, for instance, "Swimming lessons at the local pool are taught while children are off-track and others are still in school." They also indicated that their schedule permitted children to participate in activities that might not be offered in the summer, or to "have a chance to do things out in the community while others are in school." They noted that this flexibility gives the community an opportunity to "get involved with school projects and activities all year," and that this, in turn, might provide "better quality time and bonding" and "better unity" that might "make for a better community."

Parents of children on both school calendars were concerned that it was sometimes difficult in a community with schools on multi-track schedules to tell whether students were being truant or were just "off-track." However, parents of YRS children also felt the shorter breaks were associated with less delinquency and "helped to keep kids off the streets in the summertime." They also believed YRS was helpful "in small ways, like finding daytime babysitters." The parent-owner of a daycare center wrote, "It gives us the opportunity to offer a more complex school-age program."

Some felt that traditional schools resulted in all the kids being out
during the summer, with too much time on their hands, which
might result in the formation of "rivalries and gangs." Others
thought that YRS "could probably add to delinquency." A few lamented that "city recreation information for deadlines was not always disseminated to off-track students on time," causing annoy-
ing late fees and missed opportunities. It became evident that both
groups of parents expressed concerns that were similar in nature.

UNDERSTANDING THE PARENT COMMENTS

It is clear from the data that parents have pronounced opinions
concerning many aspects of their children's schooling and that the
school year calendar is a subject that generates considerable debate.
We have found that parents, regardless of the schedule, are generally quite satisfied with their children's school. When we sought to
understand how parents perceived the differences between the two
calendars in terms of advantages and disadvantages to individual
children, families, schools, and communities, we found that each
group raised similar issues. These most commonly included topics such as length of vacation, student free time, retention of learning, teacher enthusiasm, and care of school buildings.

Overall, in our study, more than 90% of parents from both traditional and year-round schools expressed "considerable satisfaction"
with their children's school experience as well as with their
children's teachers. Likewise, 80% of parents from both types of
schools indicated "reasonable satisfaction" with the amount of
homework their children received, the school administrator, the
way their school community council worked, the way their school
reported student progress, and home-school communications. The
only topic about which there was a significant difference in parental satisfaction was in the area of school breaks and vacations. Parents of children in traditional-calendar elementary schools found
family scheduling to be easier if the holidays and breaks coincided
with those of older siblings in junior high and high school.

Nevertheless, we found considerable differences in how parents
with children in each type of school perceived the issues. In general, patron comments from year-round schools seemed to have a

higher emotional content than those gleaned from traditional schools. For example, one parent from a YRS commented: "It's plain stupid! All schools need to go back to traditional schooling or build more schools. I feel the year-round children are not learning like they should." Yet, parents of children in traditional-calendar schools also expressed strong feelings, generally also about the year-round calendar. One wrote in the same vein, "What could be more disruptive to a family than having all members affected by a year-round schedule?"

On the other hand, some parents with children in both types of schools also expressed fervent conviction that year-round schooling is the best option. A traditional-calendar patron stated, "There is no other alternative to create a better learning environment than year-round and why they don't make the change is a big puzzle to me." A YRS patron supported this perception, "Why change something that is working so great? I can't understand why a pigheaded few people want to push traditional school when the school is already so overcrowded. My children are top students and are doing great with the smaller class sizes made available through year-round school. We love it!"

Parents with children in traditional-calendar schools tended to see the traditional calendar as a bastion of society. They believed it helped to protect the community as well as family activities and values. Parents of children in YRS tended to focus on what they perceived to be better and more natural learning rhythms and opportunities. Both groups were inclined to focus on the perceived benefits of their own calendars and to dismiss or refute the reputed advantages of the other calendar. There is little doubt that, despite the generally strong positive support for the three-week breaks, if parents have children in both YRS and in schools with other calendars, then scheduling of family vacations becomes more difficult.

Normally, where intersession exists, very favorable parental responses are commonplace and expected. In Delphi District, no schools offer intersession programs. The finding of a positive parental response to multi-track year-round schooling in this district showed an especially strong level of support for the YR schedule in that it was not confounded, as is sometimes the case, with support for intersession.

CONCLUSION

We have learned, as have others, that parental opinions change substantially following implementation of YRS. Although many of those who have not experienced year-round schooling seem to hold strong opinions against it, once the change of calendar has been in place for several years, many of the concerns related to student learning and family cohesiveness are alleviated. It is important to realize that much of the early hostility that is frequently expressed against year-round school will probably not be reflective of the attitude of parents or the community as a whole once the calendar has been in place for a couple of years. Except in cases where a district has made serious errors in its approach to implementation, we have found that the anti-YRS hostility dissipates after implementation.

Our research leads us to conclude that the findings of Merino (1983) still hold. Parents, in general, support whatever calendar their children are on and want to maintain it. Parents also tend to resist, and even fear, a change to an unfamiliar calendar, unless they are convinced that the new calendar will indeed hold significant benefits for their children's learning.

CHAPTER 6:

THE IMPACT OF YEAR-ROUND SCHOOLING ON TEACHERS

I'm not looking forward to it because of the kind of person I am. I use most of my summer to be ready for school for the next year. Now, I don't think I'll ever get a break. My only hope for it is that any teacher I talk to that's on year-round says they love it. (Teacher)

*****

When we had an opening last year, the teachers were allowed to participate in interviewing. After we had interviewed about 40 people, we told the principal to just finish and decide. For every opening in year-round there are at least 50 teachers in this district who want it. I heard a principal say she had never lost a good teacher back to traditional. (Teacher)

*****

Parents are frequently heard to comment that the teacher is the key to a child's educational experience. This comment is generally taken to mean that the better the teacher, the better the child's school experience and academic success. If the teacher is the key to a child's educational experience, then it stands to reason that a teacher's attitude toward an educational reform might affect how well it is implemented and whether its impact on students is positive or negative.

Fortunately, for those implementing year-round schooling, teachers are overwhelmingly positive about the innovation. Of the more than 100 teachers we interviewed or surveyed, fewer than 5% stated a preference for the traditional calendar. Although 95% preferred the year-round schedule after some experience with it, not all were so enthusiastic at the outset. Some had expressed serious pre-implementation concerns and questions. Yet, even more than for parents, a firsthand experience with year-round schooling convinced teachers of its benefits, first on a personal level, and then for what they increasingly perceived to be benefits to students.

In this chapter, we draw on our data from more than 100 teacher interviews and surveys to present an overview of teacher perceptions of, and experiences with, year-round schooling. The focus of this chapter is to give the reader a flavor of the advantages and disadvantages of year-round settings for teachers. We do not, as in previous chapters, attempt to compare the responses of teachers in traditional-calendar schools with those in year-round schools. In this case, all of our respondents had had experience with both calendars and were able to speak knowledgeably about the relative merits and disadvantages of each calendar. Because the traditional-calendar school experience is well known, there is little need for us to elaborate it here.

For teachers, there seems to be little difference between multi-track and single-track experiences. Both are clearly preferred over traditional school calendars. For the most part, we will not differentiate between responses of teachers in single-track or multi-track schools. However, where there are unique challenges and situations related to a specific calendar, they will be clearly identified.

In the research literature, there are numerous references to positive responses concerning year-round schedules, but few articles do more than give a list of possible benefits. In this chapter, we first present a very brief overview of some of the relevant literature. Then, we describe in some detail the experiences of year-round school teachers, the impact of the school calendar on their personal lives, their experiences of school organizational issues, and particularly, their pedagogical practice—how the calendar affects their reflection on, and practices related to, teaching and learning.

WHAT RESEARCH SAYS ABOUT TEACHER PERCEPTIONS

The research clearly indicates that teachers with experience in both year-round and traditional-calendar schools (TCS) are overwhelmingly positive about the relative merits of YRS compared with TCS (Brekke, 1983; Christie, 1989; Gandara, 1992; LAUSD, 1983; Merino,

1983; McNamara, 1981; Peltier, 1991; Webster & Nyberg, 1992). Some reasons for general satisfaction relate to perceptions of higher student enjoyment and motivation (Hazelton et al., 1992; Zykowski et al., 1991), higher personal levels of motivation (Shields & Oberg, 1995), and sometimes, higher salaries (Goren & Carriedo, 1986). Prior to working in YRS, some teachers express concerns about whether there will be an opportunity to complete university courses and other professional development activities. They also wonder whether there will be difficulties associated with family vacations. These concerns have been found to be unwarranted.

Some teachers reported increased opportunities for professional development (Herman, 1991) and many others indicated a preference for the resulting vacation schedule (Shields & Oberg, 1995). Especially convincing was the finding that after three years on what is perhaps the most complex and controversial MY-YRS plan, the Orchard Plan, only one of 57 teachers had requested a transfer and 95% stated a continuing preference for the plan (Gandara, 1992).[1]

LEARNING FROM TEACHERS ABOUT YRS

In the rest of this chapter, issues related to teacher perceptions concerning year-round schooling are explored by using data from our study of more than 100 teachers from several districts. Most topics are illustrated by using direct quotations taken from the teachers themselves to give a better sense of the salient issues they identified concerning YRS. During our six-year research project, we were impressed by the uniformity of the issues and concerns and the consistency of the teachers' comments and responses in the United States and Canada. This gives us considerable confidence that the following information concerning the impact of year-round schooling on the personal and professional lives of teachers is accurate and generally transferable.

The success of year-round schooling, like any other educational reform, depends on local factors related to the social, demographic, and political context of individual schools and districts. (We discuss these in detail in Section III.) In some jurisdictions, we have heard

[1]In this plan, teachers remain in school, while students actually rotate in and out of their classes.

teachers complain bitterly about how shoddily year-round schooling has been implemented, about false promises made by boards
or districts, and about hasty and, in some cases, thoughtless implementation. These have resulted in negative experiences with year-
round schooling. Yet, even in these districts, most teachers stated
that their discontent was with the methods of local implementation
rather than with the innovation itself. Of course, just because teachers are extremely positive about YRS does not mean that they see
it as being perfect; we would likely be highly suspicious if they did.
Nevertheless, it is useful to understand how teachers respond to the
YR calendar.

Teacher Attitudes and Personal Issues

When asked which calendar they preferred, not only did most
teachers indicate a preference for year-round schooling, they elaborated with considerable enthusiasm. One teacher commented at
some length,

> Well, with traditional, over the summer, my first month was spent just
> totally forgetting. I wanted nothing to do with school. Nothing. I didn't
> even want to think about it. And then, starting about the middle of July
> I'd get kind of gearing up again and my kids would start saying "Mom,
> when do you go back to work?" They got tired of me. I didn't want to
> be home anymore. And I had all these wonderful ideas and then I'd
> come back; I'd start school again and there's no way I could do it all at
> once. I'd do a few things and go gung-ho until Christmas and then
> barely make it from January to May.

Another teacher stated, "I love year-round. I was burning out so
badly in traditional. It just seemed like it was a huge splurge of time
and then all summer you're leading a different life." Both educators raised issues frequently addressed by other teachers: the impact of the calendar on their personal life, the long summer vacation, and teacher burnout.

Teachers on year-round schedules commented that if they had
children in schools with different calendars, it was a mixed bless-
ing. On the one hand, it was nice to have the opportunity to be
"Mom" or "Dad" and to see their children off to school in the morning and welcome them home in the afternoon, having had some

personal time throughout the day. However, this advantage sometimes became a disadvantage if children had to stay at home alone or when family vacations needed to be scheduled. Where teachers did not have children on different schedules, they often reported the benefits of being able to flexibly schedule vacations at non-peak times when their spouses could also be free. Being able to choose different tracks for alternate years sometimes facilitated other types of vacations and permitted easier attendance at family events such as weddings, graduations, or reunions.

One concern that was often raised by teachers about to experience a year-round calendar related to summer employment. Some teachers indicated that they relied on summer employment outside of teaching to supplement family income. Though they were concerned that the year-round schedule would have a strong negative impact, most reported they found the opposite to be the case. In some instances, flexible district policy permitted off-track teachers to serve as substitutes during their vacation periods. In addition to providing opportunity for supplemental income, the practice had several concomitant benefits that had increased the stability of many school educational offerings. Schools and students benefited from substitute teachers who knew the children, programs, and policies of the school. Teachers profited from increased communication with the school during their off-track periods. One teacher stated that when in college he had been "dead set" against YRS because of the employment issue. However, he reported that in fact, "year-round has just worked out better" because he had found regular part-time employment in a family photography business. Year-round school may provide teachers with time to add to their income by working, owning part-time businesses, or even by substitute teaching when off-track.

Despite the fact that some teachers indicated they missed the long summer, they also thought it was "really terrific" to have, for example, the "whole month of December off." Having breaks throughout the school year also helped tremendously if teachers, or other family members, had severe health problems. One teacher indicated that if it had not been for the year-round schedule, she would have had to take early retirement when she was diagnosed with lupus. Others recognized that they became bored with the "different lifestyle" of the summer months, and were more productive if their breaks were distributed more evenly throughout the year. Finally, some believed that there were times when the general public thought of teaching as an easy job because of the long summer breaks, and several teachers indicated that the year-round calendar helped them to be thought of as "more professional." Associated with the shorter summer break and the insertion of three-week breaks at various times throughout the year was the reduction of teacher burnout. One teacher (who had taught seven years on a traditional calendar before switching to year-round) stated,

> The two years I've taught on year-round, I just love teaching. I don't burn out. I know there's always a break in the horizon and I see that the kids don't burn out as quickly. And it gives me the opportunity, during that off-track time, to prepare myself to come back. I spend quite a bit of that time just reading through social studies or math, or whatever, so that I am more prepared to come back and teach.

There is strong evidence that teacher attendance is better once a school moves to a year-round schedule. Perhaps this is because teachers feel more ready to return to school. During its first winter on a dual-track schedule, one elementary school of approximately 500 students found it saved more than $20,000 in substitute teacher costs because of better attendance on the part of the year-round teachers.

Year-round schooling also seemed to offer teachers some flexibility in professional development. Several teachers told us that at the beginning of the year they leafed through the district's professional development offerings—some trying to find events that were offered when they were on-track so their vacations would not be interrupted, others selecting those scheduled when they were off-track so they would have the day to prepare, be fresher, and more able to benefit. Teachers taking university classes found, for the most part, that classes were scheduled at times convenient for them and several indicated that they "could just slide until they went off-track and then do their major papers." Despite the fact that getting a degree in this way "took a lot of dedication" and most of the "off-track time" for two years, the degree was readily achievable. Only one teacher, trying to complete a master's degree at a college offering mostly off-campus classes, found it difficult to try to schedule the required on-campus component in the summer. Ultimately, in-

tervention on the part of the school district resulted in some modification of the requirements to satisfy her work schedule.

In-service activities scheduled in the school district were sometimes perceived to be more difficult to schedule for year-round
teachers. For example, YRS teachers still on-track found it quite
difficult to take many workshops and training sessions scheduled
early in the summer when teachers from traditional schools were
on vacation. One person, in talking about this situation, described
the situation of YRS teachers as "district stepchildren." Frequently,
though, districts overcame this difficulty by covering the cost of
substitutes to enable groups of teachers from year-round schools to
attend sessions.

Overall, as one teacher described it, YRS seems to offer a more
natural and enjoyable way of living: "I think school becomes a way
of life rather than an endurance contest . . . and then you're off [for
the summer]. . . . School is a part of our life; it isn't just a big long
hang-in-there-till-its-over and then you can have fun attitude." In
other words, the rhythm of work and vacation becomes more continuous, less an uphill climb to complete the school year followed
by a long and needed period of recuperation. "I love year-round—
I'd never go back," is a sentiment frequently heard by teachers who
have experienced both traditional calendars and year-round schedules.

Organizational Issues

There is little doubt that the organization of year-round schooling
requires teachers to think differently about many of the activities
in which they traditionally engage. For all teachers from year-round
schools, there may be differences in how they relate to the wider
community in terms of activities that occur at particular times of
the year. For example, if students are not in school during Hallow-
een, they may not have an opportunity to participate in the annual
costume parade.

Districts that have a number of schools on different calendars
have to ensure that needed services are available for all schedules
and throughout the whole year. They may need to seek adjustments
to the district's testing schedule to accommodate their year-round
calendar or ensure that reports of average daily attendance are not

required during an off-track period. Sometimes district services are closed or minimal for the start-up period in the summer and teachers may not be able to access all district support systems.

Teachers who were coaches and leaders of extracurricular activities reported that they needed to rearrange their practice schedules and some had to be willing to engage in regular league or tournament events during their breaks. Some coaches addressed this issue by sharing the leadership of an activity with another teacher or a parent. Some recognized that their coaching stipend covered the entire athletic season and felt being present was just part of the job. For others, this was perceived to involve sacrifice of vacation time.

The most important adaptation for single-track teachers, either at the elementary or secondary level, is likely to be the decision of whether to teach at intersession, and if so, how many sessions they can accommodate without experiencing burnout. In some districts, where intersession programming is funded by a reallocation of summer school funding, teachers are usually paid according to the summer school salary grid. For others, where intersession is funded through special grants or supported, in part, by student fees, teachers may find they are receiving considerably less than their regular daily salary for teaching intersession. When teachers decide to teach intersession, they need to make decisions about appropriate pedagogical approaches because the sessions are frequently structured differently from regular sessions in terms of length, emphasis, and policy.

Organizational Issues Specific to MT-YRS

Teachers in multi-track schools deal with a number of additional organizational challenges that single-track teachers do not have to confront. These relate to accommodations necessary for having specific groups (or tracks) moving in or out of the school and to the communication necessary to ensure that transitions occur smoothly. There are also issues related to assignment of teachers and students to tracks and to the perceived disadvantages or benefits of different tracks. The significant issue of track composition will be addressed in Chapter 8 and is simply signaled here. Another topic briefly mentioned here (also elaborated in Chapter 8) is the impact of MT-YRS on the school as a community and on the teaching and learning environment. Teachers sometimes find that, without increased effort and planning, multi-track schools may not have the sense of cohesion or community that traditional calendar schools may enjoy.

Moving and Downtime

When multi-tracking has been implemented to enable districts to accommodate more students in existing buildings, many teachers and students are required to pack up their materials and move out of their classrooms for the three-week break and into a different room on their return. Some expressed strong dislike for this aspect of year-round schooling, especially when the designated classroom had not been properly prepared according to the agreed-on timeline or schedule. Others, after getting used to it, found they accommodated quite readily to the typical MT year-round system of assigning teachers large cabinets on wheels in which to store all of their materials. These cabinets were generally placed in an accessible storage area while teachers were off-track and then moved into the teachers' new classrooms during the track-change period. Some took great care to be ready: "I usually start preparing to go off-track in my spare time. I make sure I get everything packed up, put in closets, and stored in one area so it can be ready to move out on Friday afternoon. It doesn't really take away from the learning of the kids." One teacher, following her college graduation, approached her new assignment in a MT year-round school with trepidation. She feared having to change rooms would mean she wouldn't be able to make her room as "cutesy and all fixed up." However, following some firsthand experience with YRS, she recognized that "what happens is that you learn to organize yourself and you don't carry things around that you don't need and definitely you keep things a lot more neat, a lot more organized."

The issue of whether children lost instructional time as they prepared for a track change in multi-track schools was important. Most teachers attempted to streamline the process by scheduling a group activity, saving an educational video, using the time for testing, or for physical education. A few indicated that, despite their best efforts, there was some lost time but they felt that it was much less than the even longer periods of downtime experienced in traditional schools prior to Christmas and summer vacation.

Special Events

Scheduling of field trips, assemblies, and special events is also more complex in multi-track year-round schools. In some schools, assemblies were held twice, once to accommodate tracks A and C, and a second time to provide for students on tracks B and D. In others, teachers simply attempted to have a reasonable variety of activities for each track. Sometimes, there was no effort to make special events inclusive, as in the case of the annual symphony field trip for some schools in Delphi District. One teacher commented that she was really disappointed because the fifth grade went to the symphony every year when her track was off. Although students were invited back, many were unable to attend because of family activities. Depending on district policy, the opportunity for students to participate when on vacation is not always permitted.

Overall, access to in-school facilities and opportunity to participate in regular school activities seemed improved by most multi-track organizational arrangements. For instance, when some students were off-track, the rest experienced increased access to facilities such as the gym, library, art rooms, or computers. Playground and lunchroom supervision seemed easier. In addition, educators frequently commented on how much relief they noticed from overcrowding. One talked about the difficulty in the previous year of "just walking down a hallway with nearly a thousand kids in it on any given morning. Now I can see a real difference. Having approximately 25% of your children gone at a time makes a difference. I think it's a calmer school."

Communication and Community

Another aspect of multi-track schools is the need to develop good internal mechanisms for communication and for building a sense of community. This is because, on a MT schedule, most teachers will see colleagues who are on different tracks only 50% of the time. Some schools made regular use of email to ensure that no teacher, whether on- or off-track, failed to receive necessary information. In others, communication was more problematic: "If a major decision within the faculty is made while you're off-track, they'll try to call you and get your vote, but if you happen to be out of town or you're not home when they call, then you'll miss and you don't have a say." Many schools resolved this situation by having staff meetings for part of each overlapping track-change day, every three weeks.

Although some teachers felt there was less cohesion in a multi-track school, with fewer "treats in the staff room, fewer shared breakfasts or lunches," others suggested that developing a sense of community was not simply an issue for year-round schools, but for all schools. One teacher recalled that in her first year on a multi-track schedule she rarely saw her best friends. She recognized that some traditional schools were also very fragmented. "Sometimes the first grade won't have anything to do with the sixth grade, and the communication and the friendships are always tenuous. . . . There are so many ways to divide the school."

Informal Communication

Despite some issues related to the complexity of formal communications in YRS, teachers reported that the YR calendar seemed to facilitate an increase of informal communications—both between teachers and families and among teachers themselves. One teacher, for example, described an unanticipated benefit of the newsletter she sent home as the class was going off-track. "I always send home a newsletter right before we go off-track that says when we come back on we're going to be doing this and you could review it. I sent one home this past quarter talking about how we were going to do division, and a few of my students came back knowing how to do it."

Everywhere we interviewed, teachers reported consistent benefits. They stated that having the three-week breaks to rejuvenate themselves also led to more discussion about teaching and learning when they came back on-track. The experience described by one teacher is representative.

> I got an idea from another teacher last year to set up a government in my classroom. I was just going off and she was coming on and she had just experimented with it. We talked to each other and that gave me an idea to think about while I was off-track. I started it when I came back on. This year we go off-track together, we think things through, and we talk to each other about our new ideas. There is a lot more rejuvenation happening.

Educators we interviewed reported that year-round schedules seemed to facilitate an increase in teacher talk about teaching and learning. This collaboration also seemed to carry most teachers through the logistical difficulties of team-teaching. Though a few teachers stated that team-teaching did not work in multi-track schooling, most indicated that they could overcome the organizational challenges and implement team-teaching, frequently by using a rotation of cross-grade clusters. One teacher described a complex structure that had impressed her in a previous MT-YRS where:

> Fifth and sixth grade teamed together in math, science, and social studies in three-week units. The teachers would rotate what they were teaching as well. So one kid didn't have to have division with the same teacher for six whole weeks. If they didn't understand it from the first three weeks, they would have a different teacher for the second three weeks so they would get a different perspective on it. That worked really well but it was a major effort on those Fridays when they did track change. Everybody would get together, decide who was teaching what math class, and which kids could go together, which kids had already had what teacher. It was a ton of work. But it worked really well for that school.

Summary

We found that where teachers were determined to profit from the calendar change and were able to be creative and to reconsider how they thought about and organized much of their work, everyone seemed to benefit. We are convinced that there is some validity to the perception of many teachers that educators in year-round schools are more flexible than those in traditional schools. "If you're in year-round and you can't flex, you're in big trouble," one commented. Another agreed, "If you're not an adaptable teacher, you just better get out of year-round." Perhaps teachers simply rise to the challenge when presented with the need to reorganize or to rethink their practice. This definitely appears to be true when we approach the topic of teaching and learning in YRS.

Teaching and Learning

We have found that, for the most part, teachers believed that working in a year-round school resulted in better attendance, improved personal health, less burnout, and increased levels of communication and collaboration. Accompanying these benefits was a noticeable increase in the level of enthusiasm for teaching. "It is nice to have those breaks where I can get myself back together and get excited about school again and then I go back totally renewed and feel like my class does too." Teachers seemed to believe that students also benefit from the same advantages and are better prepared to engage in learning activities. Many teachers reported that students start back after a three-week break more refreshed and motivated to learn. They perceived that "there is more retention," students forget less, and they then need less review time than students in traditional schools.

Teachers suggested that the three-week breaks gave them the opportunity to be reflective practitioners but also believed that their students benefit as well: "I think the downtime is helpful for children to reflect and that's something everybody needs to do. We don't take time to do that." First-year teachers, especially, reported that being able to plan for nine weeks, and then to regroup, decide what had and had not worked, and then to make necessary adjustments was of particular importance to them. One commented, "Each track seems to get better and better and my discipline gets better and my lessons get better, because I try something new." All teachers said they appreciated the breaks. Another reflected,

> Just recently, in fact, I've been thinking a lot about my most productive time. And it is when I come right back on-track because I'm no longer stressed out and I have the rest I need. I find that I'm a lot more patient with my students. And maybe they're the same way, you know. They're more relaxed, too.

Teachers in YRS reported that they planned differently from when they had taught in traditional-calendar schools. Instead of teaching from A to Z out of the textbook, they stated that they planned in three, six, or nine-week units. Not only did this facilitate teaming, but teachers believed that it helped to keep them more focused on the learning objectives and material they need to cover. "You definitely have to keep a tight ship. There's no wasting time. When you come back on-track you review a little bit, but most of the time you just get right back into the swing of things. You definitely want to follow a schedule and not waste any time so that you get through your entire curriculum." Another stated, "You're "more economical. You get the work done in a hurry. You plan your time better."

Many teachers planned their time to end units before the three-week breaks so they would be able to start something new on their return. One stated that on a traditional calendar, "It is hard to really see the end up until the last two or three months before school gets out and then you realize you've got to hurry and cram all this in." Teachers in YRS found that the calendar facilitated planning. At the elementary level, teachers occasionally chose to emphasize some subjects for a nine-week period, and then others during the next session, instead of saying, "Well, I'm focusing on eleven different subjects for the whole year." This is reminiscent of discussions frequently held in secondary schools about the value of reducing the number of subjects taken by students at any one time.

The tighter planning and team-teaching also seemed to result in an improved focus for both teachers and students. Elementary teachers reported that being able to plan during the year with a specific group of students in mind was considerably more productive than trying to complete all of one's planning during the summer. Secondary school teachers indicated that where their school started earlier than others in the fall, they could establish academic routines and have approximately one month of focused instruction before students were distracted by football celebrations, pep rallies, and extracurricular activities. Teachers believed that, "Year-round school keeps the kids more focused throughout the school year"; yet they recognized that, for the tracks that continued into the summer of the traditional calendar, retaining focus could also be problematic.

Another area of accelerated performance seemed to be an increase in the amount of reading completed by students over the three-week breaks. Despite the fact that teachers often cannot officially assign work during the students' vacation period, many provided incentives for recreational reading and the completion of unique learning projects, thus providing a sort of individualized and informal intersession program.

Teachers in YRS overwhelmingly believed that they were more motivated and enthusiastic than their counterparts in traditional schools and that the same held true for their students. In addition, they identified fewer difficulties with discipline and classroom management as well as lower stress and tension among students and staff. In "March, April, and May, on the traditional schedule, those kids are just really wild and I was sick of them," one said. Year-round school "gives them a break right when they need it."

A final aspect of the teaching and learning environment of YRS relates to how well children are prepared for high school. In some areas, when we visited YRS, we were told that teachers had contacted the secondary schools into which their former elementary YR students had moved and that in each case, their students were perceived to be among the best prepared of the school's entering students. However, one teacher, also a parent, described how her own daughter had experienced some difficulty adjusting to the fact that because her high school was on a traditional schedule, she did not have the regularly scheduled breaks to which she had become accustomed.

CONCLUSION

We have seen in Chapter 4 that year-round schools can often be associated with higher academic achievement and improved nonacademic outcomes for students. Here, by presenting an overview of teacher comments and perceptions, we have demonstrated that they generally believe that YRS improves their working conditions as well as provides for better learning environments for students.

Where the implementers of YRS have not attended to social, political, or fiscal issues, teachers express concerns, but where YRS has been implemented with intelligence and integrity, teachers clearly believe that the benefits of a year-round schedule extend to their personal and family lives, their sense of professionalism, and their students' learning opportunities. Teachers repeatedly described how the YR schedule was associated with improvements in organizational and instructional strategies that had a direct positive impact on their classroom practice, primarily because it facilitated reflection and increased conversation about teaching and learning in an atmosphere that was less stressful and more motivating. One educator stated that the teachers she had taught with "had done more and were better teachers" on the year-round schedule.

YRS is not considered to be a panacea; however, despite the recognized difficulties, we have found overwhelmingly strong support. Teachers on both single-track and multi-track year-round schedules express firm convictions that YRS provides significant educational benefits for students.

CHAPTER 7:

THE IMPACT OF YEAR-ROUND SCHOOLING
ON ADMINISTRATORS

I love multi-track! It's so much fun to see. I could walk around and see which teachers were getting ready to go off cycle. I could tell which kids were getting ready to go off. Now, someone's ready to come back on and they're saying, "We've got to try this and this and this!" They pump everyone else up. (Principal)

*****

I wish we could talk the whole world into going single-track! (Principal)

*****

I don't think it's good for administrators. I think the burnout is unbelievable. I think it's the best service for kids and teachers. I think I've got a better faculty because of year-round than I would in a nine-month school; I can do a lot more. But for administrators, the burnout is there. (Principal)

*****

These quotations are representative of what most of our administrative respondents told us about year-round schooling. Principals spoke freely of its benefits for students, parents, and teachers, but also recognized that it presents particular administrative challenges related to workload and school organization. Not all thought that these additional challenges were negative; some found the complexity and increased demands exhilarating. All recognized the importance of district support.

In this chapter, we explore administrator perceptions of the advantages and disadvantages of year-round schooling for themselves, their teachers, students, and the school-community in general. The discussion, grounded in an overview of the relevant literature, is also based largely on our interviews with more than 65 school-based and district-level administrators. The 48 school principals who participated in our study each had experience with at least one year-round calendar (single or multi-track); most also had had administrative experience with traditional-calendar schools. For the most part, we allow them to speak for themselves, as they describe what they perceive to be the major advantages and disadvantages of YRS and as they identify the need for adequate district support.

WHAT LITERATURE SAYS ABOUT ADMINISTRATOR PERCEPTIONS

The literature says relatively little about the effects of YRS on administrators and rarely differentiates between their roles in single- and multi-track schools. However, it does suggest, that despite increases in administrative workload (particularly in multi-track schools), administrators who have had experience with both traditional and year-round education prefer the YRS model (Alkin, 1983; Christie, 1989; Goren & Carriedo, 1986; Hazelton et al., 1992; McNamara, 1981; Shields & Oberg, 1995; Zykowski et al., 1991).

Christie (1989) found that the principals in her study were "strong supporters of year-round school in spite of the fact that it significantly increased their workload" (p. 28). Among the strengths they identified were high teacher and student morale, better retention of learning, and fewer teacher absences (p. 26). Howell (1988) stated that to achieve such benefits, the development of a year-round school is "a sizeable administrative job. . . . It requires large amounts of analysis, judgment, planning, and leadership. Before beginning, administrators should realistically assess the large amounts of time and energy that will need to be spent" (p. 14). She found that the process from conception to implementation generally takes from one to three years. Howell further noted numerous elements that required administrative consideration, including room assignment, maintenance schedules, material allocation and storage, record keeping, assignment of teachers and students to tracks, and communication with parents, staff, and students. Although she did not differentiate, we suggest that each of these may have a greater impact in multi-track YRS.

In 1990, Serifs identified and elaborated many of the same issues and suggested some specific strategies to enhance the possibility of the continuation of YRS. Among these were the need for ongoing training and support for teachers and the opportunity for guidance personnel to discuss the scheduling implications with students and parents. Because he perceived that a "well-informed and participating public [would] most likely minimize conflict during the transition" (p. 14), he urged attention to communication through informational meetings and print materials. Some of his advice, although specifically addressing YRS, seems to apply equally well to all educational programs. For example, he advocated "continuous monitoring and periodic evaluation [to] strengthen the program, help maximize its benefits, and insure the program remains consistent with the district's pre-determined objectives" (p. 14).

Goren and Carriedo (1986) identified the need for support in the areas of school operations, maintenance, food services, custodial services, purchasing and materials, transportation, planning and research, evaluation, and testing services (p. 20-21). District support was also discussed by others (Peltier, 1991; Serifs, 1990). White (1992) indicated that districts with schools on both year-round and traditional schedules have to attend to two completely different sets of needs.

The literature also raises the issue of administrator burnout. Rasberry (1994) associated a lack of district support and the "administrative nightmare of scheduling" with increased administrator burnout. White (1992) stated that in Jefferson County, Colorado, administrator burnout ultimately eroded top-level support for YRS. However, in 1992, French conducted a comprehensive study of stress and burnout among 200 elementary school principals (100 from traditional-calendar schools and 100 from year-round schools). She found that both groups of principals reported low levels of burnout on validated measures assessing personal exhaustion and sense of individual accomplishment.

An important aspect of administrative decision making in multi-track schools is finding a way to ensure equitable allocation of students to tracks (McNamara, 1981; Serifs, 1990; Shields & Oberg,

1995). If administrators accede to parental requests for specific track assignments, it may result in an unequal distribution of low socioeconomic status (SES) and ethnic minority students on some tracks.

Goren and Carriedo (1986) report, "Experienced year-round school principals, directors of year-round school programs and national authorities universally state that the principal is the key element in the successful implementation of year-round school programs" (p. 25). Much of the literature pertaining to the administrative role in YRS supports their observations. Information provided by our respondents addresses the sometimes difficult challenges and real benefits of year-round schooling and helps us to better understand the pivotal role played by administrators.

LEARNING FROM ADMINISTRATORS ABOUT YEAR-ROUND SCHOOLING

In this section, we present the perspectives of school-based administrators under three main headings: the *perceived benefits* of year-round schooling, *administrative challenges* associated with YRS, and issues related to *district support* for administrators in year-round schools. Although we discuss each idea under one main heading, it is clear that our classifications are arbitrary.

Perceived Benefits of Year-Round Schooling

As we have seen, students, parents, and teachers report that whether the year-round schedule is a single- or multi-track calendar, one of its major benefits has to do with increased opportunities for student learning. Principals support these perceptions but widen the focus to describe a number of additional advantages for the school itself as well as for parents and the broader community.

Improved Learning Conditions

To some extent, associating year-round schooling with improved learning conditions may seem surprising, because the formal curriculum and the learning objectives are similar within a given district for all schools regardless of the calendar. We tend to agree with one administrator we interviewed who stated, "I think the key thing is back to that teacher." He explained that he would be surprised if there were major differences in learning among children with "good teachers in a good climate." Nevertheless, our ongoing research suggests that where year-round schools are successful, they tend to be associated with significant positive changes in the school's climate or learning environment.

The perceptions of the administrators whom we interviewed are consistent with those of parents, students, and teachers reported in previous chapters; they believe there are greater motivation, less stress, and more collaboration and interaction in year-round schools than in traditional-calendar schools. We frequently hear comments like, "Teachers have less burnout. The kids come back with that certain excitement. I think the students are happier in a YRS. I don't see the burnout, the tiredness toward the end of the year. I think students are happier, I think teachers are happier." Principals also maintain that there is more teacher interaction and, consistent with teacher reports, they observe that teachers are more organized and plan their instructional units differently in year-round schools.

In addition to the foregoing advantages cited in the literature, we have found several other compelling explanations for the positive climate of YRS. Some administrators have suggested that YRS requires more adaptability on the part of both administrators and teachers. Perhaps because of this flexibility, a change to a YRS calendar is sometimes a catalyst for additional changes in structuring or conceptualizing teaching and learning. In particular, when implemented, intersession enhances the learning opportunities for students.

One principal explained, "It seems like teachers are more flexible and ready to make changes because they've had to move every nine weeks." Discussing the surprising number of requests for transfer into his school following its change to a dual-track calendar, another principal stated that teachers know they are coming to "a school where people have to be flexible. You don't come here unless you are flexible, ready for changes, and I'm constantly dropping hints that change is in the wind."

To illustrate how YRS acts as a catalyst for other changes, we have shown how its implementation frequently seems to be associated with alternative structures and organizational arrangements for teaching and learning. Previously given examples include the learning communities in Stephen Lewis Junior High School, the villages introduced in St. Michael District, Super-Session in Jerico Elementary School, and the community-based outdoor education programs in some of Ontario's dual-track schools. Other changes involve the allocation of high school credits for intersession classes or the deployment of student teachers during intersession to provide intensive remedial instruction.

At the secondary level, we thought that principals would likely prefer to have their schools on the same schedule as other schools in the district. We speculated that having all schools on the same calendar might be more convenient, perhaps facilitating competitive sports schedules. On two consecutive days, we interviewed three different secondary school principals who, using almost the same words, disagreed. They stressed the organizational benefits of being on a single-track schedule while the rest of the district remained on a traditional calendar. They spoke enthusiastically about the strong academic focus achieved in the first month when such distractions as football games, initiation, or homecoming were postponed until the rest of the district had begun classes.

Intersession programs have also been reported to revolutionize the ways in which schools meet the needs of secondary students. In Chapter 3, we described how intersession offered students the opportunity to repeat classes in which they had been failing, complete classes where they had fallen behind, opt for accelerated acquisition of credits to permit earlier graduation, or even to choose enrichment classes, such as conflict resolution or music camp. These programs have been found to reduce student dropouts and enhance graduation rates in participating schools.

Intersession also frequently accompanies the introduction of a year-round school calendar at the elementary level. Principals see it as one of the major ways of promoting increased learning and overcoming the learning loss suffered by some students over the long summer vacation. Several principals of multi-track elementary schools described how their intersession programs were specifically intended to support students most in need of remediation or enrichment.

Some administrators recognized that intersession not only sustains the academic performance of students but also offers social and emotional support. One phrased it this way: "We kept them tied to school emotionally. The intellectual sometimes isn't the name of the game for kids who are having trouble." Although most educators were familiar with the multiple advantages of intersession, not all multi-track schools had space in which to accommodate such sessions. Where administrators and teachers were committed to this aspect of student learning, they had been particularly creative in finding space and financial support elsewhere. In areas where funding was not available for intersession, some schools raised money through popcorn sales, movie nights, and other fundraisers. Innovative planning for intersession also enabled schools to offer opportunities that encouraged parents to participate more fully in school life. We have previously noted how, in some schools, parents also participated in high school equivalency programs, field trips, and other intersession activities.

Although intersession is particularly easy to implement in a single-track school at both the elementary and secondary level, the additional challenges of scheduling, staffing, and space procurement mean that without effort, creativity, initiative, and commitment on the part of the school principal, it is unlikely to happen in multi-track schools. In addition to advantages related to the organization of the learning environment, increased focus, and intersession opportunities, the principals we interviewed saw other benefits to year-round schools.

Impact on the Community

In many instances, extensive consultations and meetings between school and district personnel and members of the wider community preceded the introduction of year-round schooling. These extra efforts at communication with parents and community groups frequently resulted in increased support for, and commitment to, the school and the new calendar.

In many instances, elementary school administrators described how they introduced initiatives to accompany the implementation of year-round schooling. These overtures resulted in more parent volunteers in the school, as well as remarkable numbers of parents taking advantage of new learning opportunities. For example, one principal expressed surprise that more than 200 parents had enrolled in the school's newly implemented course on parenting skills. Another noted that, "The minute you link the school and the community together, parental involvement booms."

Administrators concurred with student perceptions that at the secondary level year-round schooling did not have a negative impact on student employment. Those students who were off-track found it much easier to get full-time seasonal work because employers recognized they had their undivided commitment during the break. Employment did not seem to compete with academics because students could often reduce their hours when back in school, giving students who were then on break the opportunity to work more hours.

Principals agreed with teachers that the year-round calendar seemed to alter the impression that teachers only work part of the year. More than one administrator observed that teachers on a traditional schedule had sometimes been "embarrassed and felt guilty with summers off." This changed perception seemed to contribute to a higher morale among personnel working in year-round schools.

Some administrators reported that, by specifically inviting members of various community groups to information sessions, they were able to both garner support from, and create partnerships with, community organizations. The resultant good will often seemed to facilitate adaptations in community recreation programs, childcare provisions, shared facility use, and improved student employment opportunities. Other school administrators considered the change to a year-round calendar as a structural innovation only and did not accompany it with any significant communication or reconceptualization of the relationships between the school and its community. However, where year-round schooling was seen by the district as a temporary fix, we found much less evidence of principal initiative to increase community involvement.

School Level Benefits

School administrators perceived a YR schedule offered clear benefits for teachers. They reiterated most of the ideas expressed by teachers in Chapter 6: more flexible vacation opportunities, less burnout, increased motivation, increased reflection time, and more appropriate planning time interspersed throughout the year. One principal of a dual-track school (in which teachers and students had the opportunity to choose either the traditional or modified schedule) noted that "just having the two calendars in the school makes the teachers more enthusiastic because they think they have some control over the problems."

Many principals and district administrators believed that additional benefits accrued to schools because of increased teacher satisfaction. Several identified improved teacher attendance and concomitant decreased substitute costs. Another reported that the number of student behaviors requiring disciplinary action had "dropped dramatically" by as much as 66%. Principals of year-round schools also reported decreased vandalism in the schools, perhaps because schools were vacant for shorter periods of time.

Where school and district administrators had successfully introduced the concept of year-round schooling, a school's change to a year-round calendar was sometimes accompanied by enthusiastic media coverage. For one school with a rather negative reputation in its community, the calendar change proved to be a boon. Where teachers had previously been reluctant to move to that school, the administrator explained that as soon as word of the change in calendar was out, the press gave the school considerable positive coverage. He continued that the "good press has changed the image of this school significantly." Not only had there been improved morale, but the school received, after its first year, more than 30 transfer requests from other teachers in the district. This is consistent with the report of a principal in a different district that he had "never lost an excellent teacher back to a traditional school" and with his statement that, in his district, there were more than 40 applicants for every teaching position in a year-round school. We have found this to be true throughout North America. Wherever year-round schooling (either single- or multi-track) has been successfully implemented, teachers line up to get a position in a YR school.

Two principals we interviewed had the luxury of opening new schools on a single-track schedule before changing to a multi-track schedule in their second year. This, they each believed, was having the best of both worlds. Starting out on a single-track provided opportunities for all teachers and students to get to know each other and for the staff to develop a sense of community and some shared strategies. They were able to develop consistent approaches to attendance, discipline, homework, and intersession. Each said that when, as expected, enrollment burgeoned, the transition to multi-track was extremely smooth. Moreover, it facilitated better use of space and improved access by reducing the pressure on the public spaces, for example, the cafeteria and gym, as well as specialized areas such as the library and computer labs.

For schools and districts wanting to reduce the number of students being educated in portable classrooms, there is also little doubt that multi-track year-round schooling can reduce crowding and decrease the need for portables. In one school, the principal told us that they had had a veritable "portable city" with 15 portables. Reduction of portables was accompanied by an increased sense of unity, better communication, safer and better learning environments, and increased access for students and teachers to all of the school facilities.

We have identified issues of year-round schooling related to the learning environment, community, and the school itself. The administrator's role, in each of these, is vital. However, as described in the next section, benefits often do not occur without personal cost.

Administrative Challenges

One administrator of a MT-YRS captured a sentiment we heard frequently among principals: "Year-round school is so wonderful for teachers, but I'm going to be really honest with you; it is a killer for the administrator." This suggests particular challenges for administrators of year-round schools. Yet what some perceived as negatives, others found exciting.

Organization of the School Year

One difference of opinion related to the impact of the calendar. Although the annual opening day of a year-round school is no different from the opening of a traditional calendar school, some administrators feel pressured by the lack of a long summer period in which to plan. As the school year drew to an end, some administrators reported they missed the opportunity to bring closure or look back and see what they had done, perhaps to say, "That was a good year." This lack of closure, one remarked, contributed to administrator burnout because "there's never an ending or a beginning."

In contrast, other principals liked the cyclic nature of the calendar. One stated that in his school, students on the twelve-week on, four-week off schedule (60-20) were always entering and leaving school in a regular rhythm. The only difference, he said, was that at the end of one of the breaks, students rotated into a different teacher's classroom. He believed that this enabled his school to be truly year-round and eliminated the need for "start-up" all together.

Although not having a definite beginning or ending may be perceived differently, principals were consistent in mentioning the risk of administrator burnout as the greatest disadvantage of year-round schooling.

Stress and Burnout

The issue of stress and burnout may perhaps be best understood by a brief discussion of some of the challenges confronting year-round school principals. Single-track principals have sometimes experienced the inconvenience of trying to adhere to district deadlines that had been established for the majority of schools on a traditional schedule. However, most of the challenges in scheduling and assignment related specifically to multi-track schools. These included determining bus routes, scheduling of school space and special events, allocation of teachers to tracks, and assignment of students to classes. Administrators and districts have different perceptions and use varying strategies to deal with these issues.

Where administrators appeared to experience the most stress, they took personal responsibility for rescheduling the space at every track change. While some principals tore out their hair reassigning bus routes following every track change, others delegated the responsibility to a school committee. Still others followed district designed and established bus routes that remained consistent throughout the year. In some multi-track schools, principals described the process of scheduling areas such as computer labs, gymnasiums, or lunch times as an "administrative nightmare." However, in other jurisdictions, the schedule for the whole year for every track was established at the beginning of the year, (sometimes by a staff committee). When a track was not in session, its space was available for extra booking. Some principals were concerned with ensuring that assemblies and special events were repeated so that all students would have common experiences. For others, the concern was simply to ensure that each track had an equitable number of interesting enrichment activities.

In some districts, where there had not been sufficient early awareness of the problem, many administrators accumulated (and sometimes subsequently lost), considerable amounts of unused vacation time. One principal said that even when she agreed to take her vacation time, leaving her assistant in charge, she felt she paid for it later because, as she put it, the "public perception is the school's open, the principal has to be there." Recently, districts have become aware of these problems and have taken a number of measures to address them. These include hiring retired principals to cover for building administrators and, in an attempt to encourage principals to take their full allocation of vacation time, changing the policy to restrict the amount of time that might be carried over from year to year.

Internal Communication

The topic of internal school communication in multi-track schools was often raised. Although some principals were particularly concerned about positive interaction and tried to have everyone present for staff meetings and decision making, others held regular meetings and simply invited the input of those who were off-track.

Many principals of multi-track schools tell stories about how either they, or someone else, forgot that although school was in session, one fourth of the school population was not. One administrator described an incident in which he had failed to remind the local press of their year-round status. He had "a teacher who was recognized by one of the newspapers; they came out to present the award to her when she was off-track. It was an all too human mistake." Another admitted, "I've blown it a couple of times. It's easy to forget about the track that's off." Most indicated that after a few years, their awareness changed and communications became less difficult. They had learned how to make better use of mechanisms like email, weekly memos, and color-coded day planners to ensure they communicated in a timely fashion.

Track Assignments

Principals need to pay careful attention to the allocation of teachers to tracks. In some districts, this is an item negotiated between the union and the district. Sometimes, administrators leave the decision making to their individual staffs, feeling that teachers are willing to compromise and be flexible and can work it out among themselves. In these instances, although rarely used, having an appeal procedure in place is still desirable. In some schools, to avoid the possibility of having all of the senior teachers on one track, strategies have been developed to circumvent using a seniority system to determine track allocation. Sometimes, teachers have even drawn lots as year-round schooling was implemented. Those with first choice in one year, moved to the end of the line the next year to ensure that everyone had a first preference on a rotating basis. We learned that sometimes no procedures had been developed. Early in a district's experience with year-round education this may not have presented problems, but for obvious personnel and union reasons, not having a policy seems a perilous course of action. A clear process for track allocation is generally beneficial for all concerned. Though it may be difficult to achieve, most principals have indicated that they appreciate a policy that helps them to ensure a balance of teaching styles and experience on each track.

Balance becomes particularly challenging when the issue of student assignment to tracks and classes is added to the mix, a task that is handled differently from district to district. In some districts, where parents are asked to indicate their first, second, and third choice of tracks, principals do their best to accommodate parental choice. Parents who receive their requested track are generally pleased, although those who do not receive their chosen track often feel disappointed and sometimes discriminated against.

When an administrator attempts to fulfill parental requests, larger problems may be posed. Acceding to requests may result in an uneven distribution of students across tracks, adversely affecting both teacher morale and the potential for space savings. It may also produce an imbalance of socioeconomic level, ethnic background, and student ability on certain tracks. Other methods of track allocation may also result in serious difficulties as well. For example, assigning all of a school's bilingual, ESL, remedial, or gifted students to a specific track raises important equity issues because particular groups and programs may be "ghettoized" on the tracks that are sometimes perceived to be least desirable. Balancing programs and students with special needs across all tracks may require particular flexibility on the part of "non-enrolling" or specialist teachers. In some districts, these teachers are asked to work a four-day week for 11 months, spanning all tracks. This permits a roughly equal distribution of students from different backgrounds or with special needs on every track. Another solution chosen by some districts is an inclusive approach in which whole neighborhoods are assigned to the same track. Rather than placing students in homogeneous pullout programs, they are mainstreamed and supported in regular classrooms by specialist teachers.

Because parents tend to choose according to the teacher's reputation as well as by calendar preference, the practice of granting parental requests may result in the classes of favorite teachers on preferred tracks being considerably larger than others. This may also produce instances in which some classes and certain tracks are very crowded while others are quite sparse.

One district making the move to multi-track year-round schooling wanted to find an impartial process for track assignment. It established a lottery system that eliminated potential parental perceptions of favoritism but also reduced the principal's flexibility. A district representative, in what was described as "a sort of traveling sideshow," took a large lottery board to each school gym where all the student names and requests from that school were placed in a drum, drawn by an impartial observer, and placed on the appropriate peg.

Finally, one of the most equitable practices may be one in which parental requests to *not* have their children placed on a specific track are accommodated. This allows principals considerable leeway in terms of class and track assignment and permits more equitable distribution of students.

Morale

It is interesting that most of the principals who described these challenges and who sometimes complained about overwhelming stress and impending burnout were adamant that they had no desire to go back to a traditional-calendar school. They reported that they enjoyed the high levels of teacher morale, interaction, and professionalism, and felt that they were better able to meet the needs of their students and community. For some, there was a sense that they had the best possible staff as well as a level of district support for change and innovation that they might not have had as administrators in traditional-calendar schools. Others reported higher status within the district, sometimes accompanied by financial incentives and better political leverage with district personnel. One elementary school principal indicated that being an administrator of a multi-track year-round school was really more like being a secondary school principal than being principal of a traditional-calendar elementary school—in terms of prestige and in the complexity of job requirements.

For the vast majority, the excitement offered by the year-round school and the satisfaction gained by overcoming the unique problems and challenges far outweighed the stress and potential burnout of being a year-round school administrator. After outlining some of the difficulties, one laughed, "I'm starting to sound like a Pollyanna. Everything can be done. But I'm sold on the concept and I enjoy it."

District Support

Most school-based administrators who enjoyed the challenge of YRS recognized that the district role was critical to their success. Although district support for schools is complex and encompasses a number of areas not discussed here, there were some things principals identified as particularly important.

Most of the difficulties in the relationships between YRS and school district offices occurred when a district attempted to provide both year-round and traditional school calendars. This was especially true where year-round schooling was new and the various district services and departments were unfamiliar with its unique requirements. For example, school-opening workshops and receptions common to many districts were often held after Labor Day when traditional-calendar schools were beginning, but many year-round teachers had already been in session for several weeks. Inevitably, this led to a sense of frustration among teachers in YRS and a feeling of being "second-class citizens" whose work was less valued.

There were numerous other examples of scheduling conflicts. Timelines for ordering materials, in-district mail delivery, student support services, testing schedules, psychological assessments, and maintenance schedules all needed to be considered. For example, the traditionally accepted deadlines for reporting enrollment statistics to determine annual staffing might not be appropriate for year-round schools.

The principals of YRS we interviewed said that they needed district personnel to either have extended contracts or to stagger their vacation time to provide adequate services. Because they were open more weeks than traditional-calendar schools, year-round schools also needed secretarial services in the summer. We were repeatedly told, "Secretaries work much harder in year-round schools." In some districts additional secretarial time and support were provided to year-round schools. In others, dedicated secretaries worked overtime without compensation to complete the required tasks.

To address the problem described earlier of ensuring that principals in YRS took their allocated vacation time, districts needed to pay special attention to support in this area. Because all principals required some planning time to ensure that their schools operated smoothly, it was not enough to simply mandate that they take their assigned number of days or to expect that they would take vacations during the short breaks that sometimes occurred in the schedule. Some districts provided additional administrative allocations to YRS. This helped to address some of the workload challenges, reduced the administrator's isolation, and made it easier for a principal to be away from the building. In other districts, provision was made for retired administrators or district personnel to take over while a principal took a vacation.

Although district personnel recognized the importance of their own roles, they reported that without the skill and commitment of their school-level principals, year-round schooling would never have been successful. There was a general recognition that principals were the "gatekeepers" of the process. One district leader informed us that some principals asked to consider implementing YRS, indicated that it would be "too much work." He continued, "And they were honest about it and so I know that workload was one of the criteria that certainly caused some schools not to come forth. See, the whole process of adopting YRS in this district could have been stopped by the school administration." Even after a decision was made for an individual school to go to a year-round calendar, district people emphasized the key role of the principal. One former superintendent stated, "There's no doubt they've got to be strong. I could almost predict which schools were going to have a struggle because they did not have strong principals. All principals are not created equal."

In one region, when schools in which to introduce the year-round calendar were selected, the quality of the principal was often a primary criterion. One superintendent told us that YRS principals needed to be not only risk takers but also creative problem solvers. He stated that a principal who "needed to look in a rulebook about how to do something," would be unlikely to survive. The principal, who appreciated the flexibility offered by his district over the choice of a start date for his new YRS, exemplifies this stance. "If we can design our own calendars to suit our community, it has a chance of success. If we can't, then we know it probably isn't going to work."

CONCLUSION

There is no doubt this chapter is very positive. Perhaps it seems especially slanted in favor of year-round schooling. We have reported elsewhere that parents sometimes express strong negative feelings about YRS. We have also described how the vast majority of teachers are supporters of YRS. Administrators, despite recognizing that YRS involves some personal cost in the form of increased workload and greater challenges, still express overwhelming support because of its potential to benefit teachers and students.

We interviewed more than 65 school-based and district administrators. In each case, we specifically asked them to rate the three calendars: traditional, single-track year-round, and multi-track year-round in terms of which offered the best possible educational opportunities for students. Despite the increased personal workload, some administrators chose multi-track. A decisive majority chose single-track as the preferred schedule. Not one chose the traditional calendar.

We were surprised at this consensus because in some of these schools other people had expressed considerable discontent with YRS and a yearning for a move away from the year-round schedule. When we asked the administrators about this apparent contradiction, some explained that political factors within their community or district accounted for most of the negatives. Others advised us that these were not attributable to the year-round calendar itself but rather to its specific implementation in their district. The wide-

spread belief was that, perhaps with some specific local modifications, year-round school was still the best educational option. One
principal expressed it this way: "I see the big winners in YRS. It's
better for the kids."

SECTION III:

THE BROADER CONTEXT

In Section I, we focused on the various models of year-round schooling including single- and dual-track, multi-track, and secondary approaches. In Section II, we examined, in some detail, research related to the academic and nonacademic outcomes of students as well as the perceptions of parents, teachers, and administrators. In this section, we examine YRS initiatives in social, political, and fiscal contexts.

To do this, we recognize that public education, as we generally know it, is nested. By this we mean that it occurs for students that are in classrooms, that are located in schools, that are administered by school districts and elected boards and, in turn, that are guided by legislation instituted at virtually all levels of government. At each level, formal structures and policies as well as informal beliefs and practices influence individual schools in unique ways. In part, these are due to the distinctive geographic, cultural, and demographic characteristics of each community.

It is common to hear parents, educators, and politicians make claims for education or appeal for changes to the current system "for the good of the kids." Indeed, it seems that almost any redistribution of resources, reallocation of funding, or introduction of new programs or organizational arrangements may be justified by such an appeal. While we hope that a reasoned consideration of what is best for students in any given situation will constitute the basis for any and every educational change, we are convinced that other factors frequently outweigh purely pedagogical ones. There are so many outside pressures on educators and policy makers today that it would be naïve not to examine how some of them influence, and too frequently dominate, educational decision making. It is for these reasons that, in Section III, we address some of the overarching social and cultural, political, and fiscal considerations related to the implementation of educational change, in general, and to year-round schooling, in particular.

In Chapter 8, we focus on the nature of schools and communities in two ways. We first explore the impact that changing to a year-round school calendar has on the relationships between a school and its wider community. Then we turn to a consideration of the effects of the calendar change on the internal sense of community in year-round schools themselves. Considerations, such as quality of life, interpersonal communication, and program equity, form the basis for these discussions.

Chapter 9 situates the study of year-round schooling in a political context, recognizing that ultimately all educational decision making is political and, therefore, frequently highly volatile. We locate this chapter in both literature on year-round schooling itself and that of change theory to examine some of the stages of the initiative from initial consideration and adoption of year-round schooling, through early implementation, to continuation and institutionalization.

Fiscal considerations occupy our attention in Chapter 10. Here we examine the costing frameworks most frequently presented in the year-round schooling literature. We present and explain a framework we believe will be useful to a thorough consideration of fiscal issues as well as a relatively simple formula for a cost-benefit analysis. Key to this discussion is the concept that fiscal frameworks need to take multiple data sources and types of expenditures into consideration for true cost-benefit analysis to occur.

This section provides an overview of some of the key conceptual issues related to year-round schooling and offers some insight into how these issues play out in practical situations related to decision making and the implementation of change.

CHAPTER 8:

COMMUNITY ISSUES AND
YEAR-ROUND SCHOOLING

I'm backing year-round school, because in the long run I see it as having more benefits. Not the way that it's constructed now, but if we can get kids going to school year round, even with the breaks, perhaps eventually we'll fill in those breaks between tracks and the school will become more of a place of community, more of a place of continuous learning. (School administrator)

*****

If we could announce tomorrow that next year we're back to a traditional schedule, the community would kiss the ground of every one of those people. They feel like a red-headed stepchild—not that they dislike it so much as that we have to do it and nobody else does. (Teacher)

*****

I think they don't even notice it. I think it's been with us so long, I know this is a minute detail, but even the community as a whole with its summer sports programs, little league, and swimming, they just adapt to it and that's the way it is. (District representative)

*****

In recent years, public concern has intensified over how the neighborhood school relates to its community and its ability to develop a sense of community in the school itself. In particular, where schools are serving increasingly diverse populations in terms of socioeconomic status, ethnic mix, and student ability, the general public has taken a new interest in issues related to school culture or school community. Many schools in areas of rapid growth and increasing ethnic and socioeconomic diversity are targeted for a calendar change. In light of this, a discussion of community issues seems particularly germane to year-round schooling.

Because *community* has many definitions and connotations, we want to clarify what we mean by the term. In this chapter, we use community in two different ways. First, we examine some of the issues related to the topic of *school-community relations*. Here, community means the part of the geographic entity (town, city, municipality) that the school identifies as its neighborhood, including the families from which its students come, the parents that contribute to its advisory councils, and the businesses with which it forms partnerships. In other words, the term *school-community* refers to the school's interactions with its broader socio-political and geographic context.

Our second use of the word *community* requires more theoretical grounding. Here, we mean the culture that develops within a school itself among the teachers, staff, administrators, and students. The term is used to refer to the sense of belonging, caring, cohesion, and purpose related to the totality of the school.

There is a growing body of literature on schools as communities (Sergiovanni, 1994), as caring communities (Greene, 1993, Noddings, 1992), or even as communities of difference (Fine et al., 1997; Furman, 1998; Shields & Seltzer, 1997). These writers differ about the degree to which community implies homogeneity or requires accommodation to, and exploration of, diverse values, beliefs, and assumptions about education and schooling; nevertheless, all agree on the importance of developing a shared sense of the organization as a whole.

Other researchers have found that student engagement in learning and school life is enhanced by the degree to which students feel a sense of belonging and ownership within the school as well as an ability to make a meaningful contribution (Smith et al., 1998). It has become increasingly apparent that student engagement does not happen in a vacuum but actually mirrors the adult relationships within the organization. Thus, for example, where adults in a multi-track school find ways to overcome the possible fragmentation of track rotation, it is also easier for students to develop a sense of allegiance to the school as a whole rather than to individual classes or tracks.

Whereas a change to year-round schooling is really a structural change, some theorists have asserted that a structural change alone is not sufficient to bring about substantial organizational reform. Undoubtedly, many people faced with the calendar change to year-round schooling would be relieved to hear that the change in schedule will not necessarily be accompanied by other major changes. However, where year-round schooling is introduced as a structural modification without any concomitant changes in how people conceptualize teaching and learning or without taking advantage of the opportunity to rethink how the organization works, we have found that the change is, at best, superficial. At worst, it spawns negativity that leads to eventual failure.

Year-round schooling has the potential to improve student learning opportunities, especially when the structural change is accompanied by other reforms. Fullan (1993) makes the point that "changing formal structures is not the same as changing norms, habits, skills, and beliefs" (p. 49). Instead, he suggests that we need to *reculture* rather than *restructure* schools[1] to increase the "personal commitment to learn" that is characteristic of a "community of learners" (p. 63). He elaborates some of the concepts that underlie meaningful structural change by stating that restructuring is about "forging links to new ideas and new practices" (p. 60) and altering the ways in which people relate to one another. It provokes questions of power and involves "learning to manage and maintain change over time, among many people, and in many areas of action" (p. 61).

The literature reports that the implementation of year-round schooling has resulted in little change or disruption to community activities. For instance, summer recreation leagues and camps have reported few adverse effects (Zykowski et al., 1991) and daycare providers have made accommodations to ensure that YRS does not become a problem (Peltier, 1991). While a few organizations have protested the introduction of year-round schooling, others have voluntarily modified their programs or schedules. Most community groups seemed willing to accommodate YRS, believing that the results were mutually beneficial. Several authors (Brekke, 1983; Merino, 1983) noted a reduction in vandalism and juvenile crime.

[1]We find the framework of culture and structure very useful; however, we have some reservations about Fullan's approach. These reservations are discussed in our conclusion.

Other writers reported that YRS personnel had better contacts with community groups than they had had previously (Hazelton et al., 1992).

In the rest of this chapter, we examine the ways in which both single- and multi-track year-round schooling can help to forge links to new ideas and practices related to the development of better community relations. Before discussing the topic of in-school community, we deal with issues that pertain to schools' relationships with their wider communities.

YEAR-ROUND SCHOOL AND COMMUNITY RELATIONS

In an earlier chapter, we discussed the need to help families thoroughly understand the adjustments necessary under a new calendar. Here, the focus is on the mutual adaptation required for a year-round calendar to operate with minimal disruption to both the school and its community. In general, relations with the wider community are no different for year-round schools than for traditional-calendar schools. However, adequate initial communication is necessary for a community to understand the new calendar and consider its implications for childcare providers, student employment, community associations, recreation facilities, and the business community.

Communication and Understanding

In our interviews with personnel in schools and district offices, respondents described at length their initial strategies to communicate about a calendar change. Administrators repeatedly told us of holding numerous meetings with community groups, service clubs, the business community, and parents. In one instance, we were told of an information meeting at which the possibility of a change to a year-round calendar was thoroughly discussed. At the meeting, participants were invited to help design the actual calendar change, making decisions about when school might start and when to insert additional vacation breaks to suit the needs of their community. At the end of the meeting, participants were asked to vote on whether to investigate further. The superintendent stated, "Under those conditions, every hand went up."

In another community, a school board member and a parent approached the principal asking him to explore year-round schooling. The principal established a "dream team" made up of 12 people from the community, including the school staff, a school board representative, a parent, the president of a neighboring school council, and another school administrator. Together, they brainstormed and proposed a calendar to suit their community's needs. This was followed by a series of monthly meetings and newsletters sent to the community, so that when public meetings were held, "the group grew each time." This resulted in a series of lively meetings in which dissidents wanting to "vigilantly protect their community" were encouraged to express their concerns. Open communication and a willingness to listen to all viewpoints ultimately achieved consensus and commitment for the concept of year-round schooling.

In other districts, in which preliminary investigations into the feasibility of YRS also involved public consultation, administrators spoke about the challenge of providing accurate information. In a few cases, we were told that having to correct misinformation had placed the district representative chairing the meeting in the uncomfortable position of appearing to be an advocate rather than an impartial investigator. Other administrators agreed that the presence of an outside expert, perceived to be unbiased and trustworthy, had been of particular assistance to them.

Where year-round schooling is seen to be mandated without adequate exploration and community involvement, there is likely to be increased opposition and, sometimes, ongoing dissatisfaction. We have learned, however, that discontent can sometimes still be overcome when a contact person subsequently takes steps to improve communication with the community. One person we spoke to told us how:

> In one school where year-round was almost a forced issue and they didn't have the buy-in from the teachers and community, parents fought like crazy over issues like, "How am I going to take care of my child?" But, when we took the vote a couple of years later, these parents were more in support than those from any other school.

The importance of community consultation and communication cannot be overstated. If a community does not acquire a sense of pride and ownership in an educational reform, especially one as significant as the change to year-round schooling, its implementation and ultimate success will be seriously compromised.

Implications for Community Life

We have found that adequate communication involves helping people such as realtors, daycare providers, and recreation association representatives to understand the proposed change. When they understand it, they sometimes make modifications to their programs that help the community to adapt successfully to YRS. Parents found that most daycare providers were willing to adjust their schedules and that being able to distribute the costs for the same number of days over the whole year, rather than accumulating them in the summer, was beneficial.

Parents reported that although some community groups adjusted their schedules to accommodate the new school calendar, the lack of flexibility on the part of other community organizations presented increased challenges to their families. For example, in one community, the city adapted its recreation program to coincide with school breaks. The recreation director described it as an opportunity to expand the program by offering activities such as swimming lessons, basketball, crafts, and other programs in three-week blocks. However, in other communities in the same district, parents expressed frustration that multi-track year-round schooling had made student participation in community activities much more difficult because the people in charge had chosen to ignore the calendar change.

Although adaptation does not always occur, our respondents believed that with appropriate involvement early in the planning process, community groups were usually willing to change. One superintendent indicated that:

> One of the biggest things that we have heard from other school districts that have already been on year-round schooling for a number of years is that your community will change to meet your needs. We had a meeting and we were lucky enough to have the director of Parks and Recreation there, and he basically stood up and said, "We're here to serve our community. If you're in school, we're going to move our calendar to adjust to the times where you need the support."

The administrator added, "That was all that needed to be said that night."

In another community, parents learned that the year-round calendar was particularly advantageous to children of divorced or separated parents. An illustration was given of a judge reconsidering custody orders to reflect the year-round school calendar. We were told judges made comments like, "Now we'll change this. The child is year-round. During this three-week session, or at Christmastime [or whenever he has a break], he can spend time with Dad." The perception was that it offered more opportunities for children to be with both parents on a more regular basis than having to fit in visits during the extended summer vacation period.

Unanticipated benefits also included an apparent decrease in juvenile crime and community vandalism. Principals told us that police statistics indicated that juvenile crime rates typically skyrocket in the summer. However, they have found that where there are year-round schools, crime rates are generally lower. This may be because vacation periods are shorter and students are less bored. There are also fewer students hanging around neighborhoods or business establishments at any one time as well as shorter periods of time when children and youth are left unsupervised. In one junior high school, the principal told us that a local police officer had come to the school early in the year and asked, "What's happening around here? Usually I'm called out regularly to the school, and this year, I have only been here once." With the opening of this new school on a year-round schedule, the occurrence of juvenile crime within the community had decreased significantly. In a similar vein, the principal of another school told us that although he knew the fire marshal quite well, he had not seen him in the school in more than a year. "Usually," he said, "the fire department is up here two or three times because there are fires being set somewhere in that park or somebody has pulled an alarm." He added that the fire marshal had told him the YR schedule seemed to have had a positive impact.

A striking report of how a calendar change affected school-community relations is the following story told by another school principal:

One of the goals that we really wanted in this school was to change its public image. The most remarkable story I have is this. At the beginning of the year, when we were going to begin the modified calendar, a real estate agent in the community phoned and his words were, "What in the blank-blank is going on at that school?" And when I asked him why, he said that usually he had people coming asking not to be in this area and now he had a whole group of people wanting to move here.

The communication and consultation process had changed the public perception of the school to such an extent that, in anticipation of the dual calendar, enrollment had increased significantly. While the implication may be that people were particularly interested in YRS, it is more likely that the opportunity for community members to feel some ownership in the school program had resulted in an improved relationship between the school and its wider community.

In some instances, lack of clear communication may result in misunderstanding and unwarranted concern. In a summer resort area, although the educational community thought the planned year-round calendar would be great, the business community was apprehensive about its impact on the availability of student employment during its busy tourist season. They soon learned that the calendar change would not adversely affect student employment because, in that community, the YRS calendar was only intended for the elementary school. Conversely, it positively affected the summer availability of adult employees because they were now able to take family vacations during the rest of the year without taking their children out of class.

It seems clear that where there is open communication and an opportunity for people to feel part of the decision-making procedures, a calendar change may actually enhance school-community relations. On the other hand, if a calendar change is accomplished through mandate or in situations in which trust and open communication are lacking, school-community relations are likely to deteriorate.

COMMUNITY WITHIN YEAR-ROUND SCHOOLS

We have found that the process of changing to a year-round school calendar is most effective if it includes input from many of the groups represented in the wider community. Where parents and community have input into the design of the school calendar, they tend to support a calendar that has been designed by them and for them. Sometimes this results in increased parental involvement in the daily school program. Sometimes the payoff is an augmented sense of community within the school itself as in the explanation provided by one principal we interviewed:

> I think it's a real model for using community. I'm talking about the teachers and other staff members, and administration—bringing them together in a real collaborative model. And also a visionary kind of model to say, "Where do we want to be? What are we looking at? What are things that we would like to see happen?" And then to see those things happen. But having community involvement every day, parents in classrooms helping—parents who are artists teaching art, parents who are engineers teaching pre-algebra to the children. It's exciting!

On occasion, a calendar change has been accompanied by a sense of feeling special or important that has brought the whole school together in a new way. The media attention afforded students who returned to class early in August or who remained at school through the month of July has sometimes helped to develop this sense of cohesion and uniqueness. Sometimes, as in the case of the dual-track schools, the group that started school first on the modified schedule formed a cohesive sense of community across grade levels that persisted throughout the academic year.

It is generally accepted that teaching can be a very solitary and isolated profession. There is considerable truth to the dictum that administrative control and the impact of policy stop at the classroom door. Once teachers enter their rooms and close the doors, they are in worlds of their own making. This helps to explain why the writers mentioned earlier believe that there is a strong need for schools to become more community-like. While this requires a greater sense of cohesion and caring for one another, it also assumes a reduction in the isolationist stance of teachers and a desire to engage in increased collaboration and interaction. A change to a year-round calendar may help to overcome these problems and create a more positive learning environment. This may be due, in part, to the increased interaction that often occurs as teachers move on and off track and to the heightened awareness of the need to work together to ensure good communication throughout the year.

The sense of in-school community may sometimes be fostered because the school on a unique calendar feels isolated from district expectations and guidelines. Sometimes, successfully overcoming difficulties posed by restrictive district or union policies draws a staff together. Although these may affect any school, most of the difficult issues associated with the development of a sense of community relate to multi-track YR schools. These schools present particular challenges for educators who want to create a sense of unity within the school, to overcome potential conflicts, and to ensure equitable practices for all.

A quick re-examination of the school year calendars shown in Chapter 2 reminds us that there are really no days in which all teachers and students are in school at the same time in a MT-YRS. In fact, for a four-track schedule, those on a given track are in the school only 50% of the academic year with those from any other track. Although this situation may serve to reduce overcrowding and eliminate some tensions, it also makes interpersonal and professional communication and the development of agreed-on shared goals, vision, and collaborative school culture more difficult.

Some MT-YRS have instituted regular faculty meetings on track-change day when most teachers may be in school. Because teachers going off-track are preparing for their upcoming vacation and those returning are concerned about setting up their classrooms and being ready for students, considerable commitment to creating a sense of community is required.

The creation of community in multi-track schools involves developing an allegiance both to track and to the whole school. As we described previously, some administrators addressed this issue by implementing structures and ensuring times for both vertical (whole track) and horizontal (grade-level) integration. In each case, provisions were made to foster both types of communication. Common teacher planning times, across tracks, also helped to ensure grade-level communication. Teacher retreats, administrative team meetings, and staff social gatherings were particularly important to the development of a school wide sense of community.

Some administrators expressed a belief that it was important to monitor the competition among tracks so that rivalry did not destroy a sense of belonging to the school as a whole. They thought that if negative rivalry developed, it might result in divisiveness and unhealthy exclusivity, for instance, on the playground. On the other hand, a degree of healthy competition between tracks might foster team spirit and increased levels of participation in school wide activities. We heard how an idea, started in one track, frequently took hold and expanded to other tracks as well. Some examples included notices sent out to parents summarizing the "week at a glance," special recognition of students who had read their first books, use of student agendas to enhance their organizational ability and planning, and parent meetings being held in homes in the community. To foster a sense of school wide community, administrators needed to guard against becoming identified with any particular track. Indeed, one principal observed, "that's the danger because the community always sees who might be getting a little edge."

Thus, leadership of a multi-track school often requires a careful balancing act. We have earlier discussed the need for communication with, and feedback from, the wider community as a means of building support for YRS. Many jurisdictions have mandated school advisory councils designed to bring decision making closer to individual schools. Frequently, this council is seen to be the body through which the general public has access to, and participates in, school-based decisions.

While these councils play an important role in building support for a school and for permitting input from parents and community members, they are often mechanisms through which those members of the wider community with the greatest resources (education, social status, wealth, and time) exercise both control and power over the local school. Where such councils make decisions related to the organization of year-round schooling, school-based educators and members of the community at large also need to pay careful attention to attendant equity issues. For example, in some schools with high numbers of students from visible minority families, advisory councils may still be composed primarily of Caucasian parents. Although one way to ensure more equitable decision-making might be to provide formal representation for all groups in school decision-making bodies, proportional representation may be both a difficult and daunting process. In and of itself, such representation may still not guarantee that all perspectives or interests are heard. Some people need to be coached and encouraged to participate in public meetings; others will only be available at nontraditional times; and still others may be more comfortable with meetings held outside of the school building. For some, providing interpreters or childcare may be necessary.

All of these factors and many more come into play when decisions are made that may affect the sense of in-school community. One example is the allocation of programs and teachers to tracks, as well as students to classes and teachers on specific tracks. For instance, where parental choice determines placement and where a particular track is perceived to be the least desirable, then those parents who are the most articulate and knowledgeable about the school may have an unfair advantage. In MT-YRS, where inequities unbalance track composition, tracks may become a form of de facto segregation or streaming based on race, socioeconomic status, or academic ability. Besides being prejudicial to individual students, this type of imbalance is also detrimental to the creation of a sense of whole-school community.

A number of additional issues are suggested by this discussion. In earlier chapters, we have shown that sometimes there is better academic achievement in year-round schools than in traditional calendar schools. We have also discovered that many YRS teachers change how they plan and organize instruction. Thus, it becomes particularly important to avoid situations in which the students with the greatest academic need are placed with the weakest teachers or in the least challenging programs. For instance, in some junior high schools, we found all ESL students assigned to one track. This reduced their opportunity to move into other programs, even from year to year, and afforded them fewer opportunities to practice English with classmates who were native English speakers. It also had the effect of leaving little time in their schedule for enrichment activities or interesting electives and, thereby, may have limited their future academic choices. In addition, it effectively restricted the students to one social group.

Sometimes, to avoid creating such inequitable situations and to promote the possibility of a strong sense of community within a school, it may be necessary for a principal to buffer the school from some of the demands and pressures of its most influential parents or even its own decision-making bodies. Track assignments, bus routes, participation on parent advisory councils, assistance with special events or fund-raising are all areas in which equity may be held hostage to power and status. To resolve these matters, it may be necessary to use decision-making processes that do not always involve taking a vote. Instead, it may be useful to achieve consensus by exploring alternate community perspectives through a variety of consultative mechanisms. This may require considerable energy to bring together people from disparate backgrounds and to create a forum in which free and open dialogue may occur. It will certainly necessitate taking time to develop a climate of trust in which people may be willing to take the sometimes risky step of publicly expressing an unpopular or unexpected opinion. At times, it will demand difficult steps be taken to change the ways in which decision making occurs at a given school. Where the leadership for such changes is not forthcoming from school or district leaders, it will be incumbent on community members to ensure democratic and equitable practices. Democracy, of course, does not always involve a majority decision but sometimes needs to take measures to avoid what some have called "the tyranny of the majority." Conversely, a few powerful and vocal people, who may be in the minority, cannot be allowed to hold democracy hostage.

CONCLUSION

Creating a sense of community in a YRS as well as in the wider community involves a dual effort including new structures as well as attention to central issues of teaching and learning. All depend on what Fullan (1993) has called *reculturing*—establishing unique ways of communicating that ultimately develop new and equitable bases of support for a school as well as shared understandings about the school's fundamental purposes and its relationship with the community.

One starting point may be to develop mutual understandings around the principle of lifelong learning that might help all members of the school community to understand that learning occurs in the home, at school, and in the wider community and whether students are on-track or off-track. Indeed, this notion is fundamental to the development of learning communities—communities that are continually expanding their capacity to create their future (Senge, 1990).

Reconceptualizing the nature of teaching and learning leads to an examination of issues related to power, to an identification of the voices that are heard and excluded from the decision-making processes related to every aspect of the life of the school. Henderson and Hawthorne (1995) state:

> At issue here are the hierarchical tactics used to disenfranchise others. At issue is the lack of regard for cultural democracy, for dealing openly and honestly with the issues, for an ethic of caring in the conduct of deliberation, for engaging in inquiry to obtain comprehensive and pertinent data, and for engaging in collaborative problem solving with people of differing perspectives and understandings. (p. 103)

Acceptance of these principles may lead to a critical examination of the structures that sustain them, such as mechanisms for communication and opportunities for interpersonal interactions. For example, a staff might consider how to direct communication simultaneously to those in a year-round school and to those outside it, whether these are teachers and students who are off-track or members of the wider community. Although traditional methods of communication (newsletters or phone trees) may be useful, the use of electronic communication techniques (email or electronic bulletin boards) or large signs outside the school may also provide immediate and interactive ways of uniting those on- and off-track. Here again, the issue of power and disenfranchisement must not be overlooked, for communication with the wider community will need to be structured to include those who have their own computers and modems, as well as those who do not. Enlisting the help of local businesses, libraries, and community service agencies might help the school to establish a wider sense of community while ensuring that no members are disenfranchised. Careful attention to appropriate communication strategies and making good use of multiple methods of communication may help to foster a sense of unity within the school community.

It appears that what is needed for the creation of community in a year-round school is similar to what is needed elsewhere: the enactment of shared understandings concerning the best possible educational practices. As in other schools, this may require new forms of leadership, shared governance, the inclusion of a greater number of partners, the empowerment of students, and commitment of the wider community. Although a traditional-calendar school may be able to sustain itself without active community support, the favorable implementation of a year-round school and its continued success often depend on the strong support of the wider community and the creation of an effective school-wide culture.

CHAPTER 9:

POLITICAL CONSIDERATIONS AND YEAR-ROUND SCHOOLING

Typically, school districts do an excellent job of conducting feasibility studies, gathering research and evaluative information, organizing implementation committees, solving logistical problems, and developing communication plans. Where we often fall down is on the political side of the equation. As educators, we often assume that all we have to do is develop a good idea and tell the community about it. We neglect to recognize or act on the understanding that educational change is a political struggle, a discussion, or a debate; at its worst it is a destructive battle over what is important to people or perceived to be important to people. (McDaniel, 1993, p. 4).

*****

This consideration of year-round schooling is not just an examination of a specific school calendar but is tied in significant ways to the norms, values, and traditions of the cultures and communities within which schooling occurs. This is because schooling is, to a large extent, inseparable from the political community within which the school exists. *Political* comes from the Greek word *polis* meaning city. For the Greeks, the *polis* did not refer just to a geographic entity but to the totality of the public affairs of the community and its citizens, including its associations, values, beliefs, and traditions. In a democratic *polis*, such as Athens, the governance structures and decision-making mechanisms involved discussion, deliberation, and debate that took into account public opinion and varying perceptions. In the Athenian democracy, all public decisions made in the community, or *polis*, were by definition, political.

In this chapter, we explore the political nature of decisions related to YRS. Politicization begins in the context that provides the impetus for change, continues through the decision making that leads to its implementation, and extends into the processes that support or inhibit the successful institutionalization of the calendar change. We ground our discussion in an overview of the relatively scant literature related to the political nature of year-round schooling.

FROM THE LITERATURE

Several authors write about the political nature of modifying a school calendar. McDaniel (1993) lists a number of specific strategies for dealing with the political nature of implementation. He suggests that it is necessary to access your district and community, get a commitment from policy makers, and "approach year-round education as a political campaign" (p. 8). Donato (1996) describes the politics underlying resistance to the mandated implementation of year-round education for the children of Californian migrant workers without consultation or consideration of their unique needs. Perry (1991) and Stiff (1986) indicate that policy can have an impact on the implementation of YRS. Greenfield (1994), in a discussion of the complexity of changing to YRS, posits the need to appoint a change facilitator to help with reform related to modifications in structures and in instructional approaches. Other articles constitute evaluation studies commissioned by districts wanting to assess the effectiveness of their policies and practices (Alcorn, 1994; Atwood, 1983; Christie, 1989; Goren & Carriedo, 1986; Shields & LaRocque, 1997).

THE POLITICAL NATURE OF EDUCATIONAL CHANGE

To highlight the political nature of educational change processes, we have chosen to organize this chapter into sections that are generally based on the stages identified by change theorists. We begin the discussion by recognizing the importance of the context within which educational change occurs. We then adapt the framework outlined by Fullan (1991) in which he says that there are three broad phases to a change process. Phase one, which he states is variously labeled as initiation, mobilization, or adoption, "consists of the process that leads up to and includes a decision to adopt or proceed with a change" (p. 47). We have called this phase *conceptualization and initiation*. Phase two, as described by Fullan, is the phase that "involves the first experiences of attempting to put an idea or reform into practice" (p. 48). We use his term *implementation* for this phase. The third phase refers to "whether the change gets built in as an ongoing part of the system or disappears by way of a decision to discard or attrition" (p. 48). We use the words *institutionalization and continuation* to refer to this phase.

Although we adopt the stages identified by Fullan (1991) as one way of thinking about change processes, we recognize that this is not the only way to discuss educational reform. Nevertheless, we find the model useful for helping to organize our thinking about the introduction of year-round schooling. Before we consider each stage in turn, we briefly discuss the impetus for, and contexts of, the most recent wave of year-round schooling in North America.

The Contexts of YRS in North America

In the past few decades, many school districts throughout North America have faced significant demographic changes, resulting in part from changing patterns of employment and immigration. Accompanying these changes have been renewed political pressures for fiscal accountability and improved educational outcomes. Districts have been urged to demonstrate that their academic programs result in success for students across all socioeconomic and ethnic groups and to identify new approaches that might promote higher levels of scholastic achievement. A parallel pressure for fiscal accountability stresses the need for efficient and equitable spending in a time when, in many districts, financial resources have been declining. Thus, districts have been confronted with the necessity to house children in classrooms more rapidly than school buildings may be constructed as well as to find more cost-efficient ways to provide excellent educational programs. Thus, pressures for academic as well as fiscal accountability have led to investigations into, and often implementation of, various forms of year-round schooling.

The Academic Context

Sometimes when schools or districts are experiencing low test scores and they are pressed for increased accountability, they turn to single-track year-round schooling in the hope that it will offer a quick solution to their problems. As we have seen, most secondary school programs that employ single-track calendars design them to provide opportunities for repetition of courses failed, catch-up when students have fallen behind, or enrichment opportunities to accelerate progress toward graduation. Academically troubled elementary schools that have been ordered to find ways to improve student performance sometimes introduce year-round schooling with intersession programs to provide additional remediation and enrichment opportunities for students.

In some areas, year-round schooling has been designed to respond to specific needs or desires of the local community. In other areas, people have simply decided that the "agrarian calendar" is outmoded and does not suit their lifestyles. They may then begin to consider an alternative calendar as a way of modernizing their approach to education.

The Legislative Context

Where overcrowding has occurred, fiscal policies and constraints have, at times, provided the impetus for year-round schooling. Sometimes, even where new school construction may have been approved, jurisdictions have chosen multi-track year-round schooling rather than face the alternative—bureaucratic red tape and the several-year process of acquiring the appropriate authorizations and building permits[1] before new construction may begin. Sometimes, local ability to float new bond issues to provide for school construction is restricted to a specific percentage of a district's annual budget. On occasion, this constraint has also prompted districts to choose multi-track year-round schooling (instead of extended days or split sessions), when they have been unable to wait for several years to raise the necessary funds for new construction.

[1]One example is the Leroy Greene Lease Purchase Act, 1976, California in which the construction process was so slow and complex that it took from three to five years from initiation to the occupation of a new school.

Some districts have implemented YRS in response to legislative incentives. In California in 1983, a bill was passed that provided financial assistance to overcrowded districts, with $25 offered for "each student attending a year-round school established to reduce overcrowding" (Zykowski et al., 1991, p. 18). A few years later, in 1988, this was increased to a minimum of $125 per student for districts with at least "30% of their K-12 students in year-round programs" (p. 18). As in California, the Utah legislature also provided an impetus for YRS by informing districts experiencing overcrowding that funding for new schools would only be forthcoming if districts had first developed other forms of efficiency calendars.

The Electoral Context

In some areas, the political context effectively constrains the possibility of educational change. Where the change relates to a school calendar, such as year-round schooling, legal requirements that a school be open for a specific number of days or that education occur between certain dates (a bookend clause) may inhibit the exploration of alternative calendars.

More broadly, the political context, in which school board members and sometimes the superintendent of schools are elected, mitigates any long-term educational change. In his analysis of a YRS consultation process in central Canada, Weiss (1993) noted that the timing of the election had played an important role in the decision not to proceed with year-round schooling. In Florida, many school districts have elections every two years for both school board members and the superintendent. There, YRS became an obvious issue in election campaigns, with those who were opposed challenging advocates of YRS on a number of grounds. Although it might be difficult to argue that the YRS issue alone directly affected the outcome of any election, we have seen that newly elected members frequently began to dismantle or to undermine existing year-round school programs. The frequency with which elections were held and the need for senior officials to respond to public pressure increased the politicization of educational reform. In this climate, innovations seemed to have little opportunity to be supported, implemented, and assessed before they became fodder for another electoral campaign.

Summary

Although not all districts face the situation of biennial elections, most experience political challenges related to garnering support for major innovations. As increasing emphasis is placed on consultation with parent and community groups and on site-based management, questions may be raised concerning who should actually have a voice in decision making and how to ensure equitable and consistent implementation of decisions once they are made.

CONCEPTUALIZATION AND INITIATION OF YEAR-ROUND SCHOOLING

One of the first issues in the conceptualization of a move to year-round schooling is the need to develop a politically and educationally sound rationale that is appropriate for a specific context. This includes clarifying the vision for YRS and determining the expected benefits of the reform without making any unwarranted guarantees or promises.

The specific calendar and implementation plan selected need to be appropriate to the goals the community wants to achieve. For example, it would not make any sense to implement a single-track year-round school program throughout a district if the goal were cost-effectiveness. Where single-track year-round school is instituted, the cost per pupil of the regular education program remains relatively constant, although additional expenses may be incurred if intersession is offered. Likewise, it does not make sense to implement multi-track year-round schooling if there is not a situation in which schools are overcrowded and additional space needs to be found. Furthermore, there is little likelihood of any form of year-round schooling becoming a viable political option if its advocates are only interested in the potential cost benefits without a concurrent investigation of how the YR calendar might be organized to provide accompanying educational benefits. However, where a community has been led to expect an immediate, significant, and positive impact on achievement, no amount of information about fiscal savings alone can convince them to continue to support YRS without evidence of accompanying academic benefits.

In some instances, year-round schooling has been implemented as a temporary response to overcrowding without any thought being given to its potential long-term benefits or to building support for the change. In other areas, district personnel promised that a move to YRS would not only save money but would result in immediate and demonstrable improvements in student achievement. Motivated by educational as well as fiscal concerns, one large, influential, urban district introduced a five-year strategic plan for all of its elementary schools to move to a year-round schedule. When the results of student testing in the first year failed to show the promised achievement benefits, many constituents were disillusioned and soon opted to return to the traditional calendar.

To alleviate the potential danger of creating unreasonable expectations about year-round schooling, we have found that some districts engaged in consultative processes with their communities. These were instrumental in building support, and ultimately in gaining agreement, for proceeding with year-round schooling. In some cases a school-based committee was involved in preliminary decision making; in others, the wider community participated in initial information meetings and decision making.

Consultation Processes during Initiation

Illustrations of successful consultations have been presented in previous chapters. A further example is the case of Centennial District that started with one elementary school and then, in the following year, added a middle school and its three feeder elementary schools, for an eventual total of five multi-track YRS. The district contact person, an assistant superintendent, reported that he and interested school-based educators had engaged in extensive planning, from offering intersession (for enrichment and remediation) to providing an innovative daycare program. He had purposely invited members of specific community organizations, such as the directors of local community recreation services, to numerous public meetings to build support for year-round education.

Often, faulty initiation processes have been responsible for the failure to explore a decision to implement year-round schooling (even on a pilot basis) where it might have been warranted. In several Canadian provinces, quite extensive district investigations ultimately led to the rejection of year-round schooling. In an analysis of one experience, Weiss (1993) found that "over the course of the consultation process [a] sense of purpose was forgotten" (p. 53). As the initial purpose to alleviate overcrowding was lost, the investigation seemed to extend to a discussion of the viability of year-round schooling for all district schools, rather than focusing on the needs of those that were, or would shortly be, affected by "space and accommodation problems" (p. 54). His investigation also revealed that although ownership of the process was vested in several local board members, it did not extend to the principals who would actually be charged with the implementation of the reform. Moreover, he identified the difficulty of having someone internal to the conceptualization process considered to be the resident expert, rather than using the resources of an outside and independent authority.

Similarly, in their assessment of the British Columbia project designed to investigate YRS, Shields and LaRocque (1997) found that lack of clear goals, the need for an outside expert, difficulties in ensuring appropriate representation from stakeholder groups, and problems with sense of ownership were also related to the failure of the initiation stage. In fact, no district proceeded to implementation. They stated, "From the beginning of the YRS Study Project, there was confusion and lack of clarity regarding the goals of the project, the criteria for participation, accountability measures, and the district procedures which were to be followed" (p. 6). There were, at the outset, no guidelines about what district demographic characteristics would make YRS a suitable option for schools and no policy distinctions drawn between single-track and multi-track year-round schools. Attaching cost estimates for funding multi-track year-round schooling in particular schools with accommodation problems could have helped to avoid confusion.

Some British Columbia districts reported they were "on their own" when forced to respond to questions and concerns about YRS. This was especially true when members of the district committee felt the need to respond to inaccurate information presented by members of a vocal opposition. This supports Weiss' (1993) conclusion that sometimes an outside expert may be of considerable assistance in helping to move an exploratory process beyond initial polarized political stances. Having an impartial authority may prevent district committees from being forced into the position of appearing to be advocates and permit them to be more open about their own questions and concerns regarding the feasibility of YRS.

Representation During the Initiation

The issue of appropriate consultation and representation is especially relevant to the initiation stage of any reform. One sure way to defeat support and dampen enthusiasm for educational reform is to mandate a change from the top without giving people a part in the decision-making processes. Moreover, the obligation to include representatives of stakeholder groups in decision-making processes is more than just the most efficient way to bring about desired results. Representation is a moral imperative, although that aspect is not always clearly understood.

Representative committees are often used to promote just and inclusive decision making. However, it is sometimes possible for representatives of one particular stakeholder group to unfairly dominate a decision-making process. For that reason, it is important to ensure that representation be fair and equitable and that no one group or individual be allowed to control any aspect of the process. This is not an easy task, for sometimes the appointed representatives of specific groups may not represent the range of opinions of the group as a whole. Sometimes, a district or funding agency, that might be expected to take clear leadership of the reform process, abrogates its own leadership role out of fear of appearing undemocratic. This is a danger to be avoided because, without appropriate leadership, the strongest and most powerful voices may dominate the voices of reason and expertise, and micro-concerns may be allowed to take precedence over the good of the whole. As can be seen, the leaders or moderators of a consultative process have an extremely difficult balancing act to perform if they are to provide a forum for the free and open exchange of ideas that also ensures protection for important minority concerns.

On occasion, the composition of a consultative committee may be designed to effectively silence and marginalize members of constituent groups who may have divergent perspectives or interests, just as it may be a way of providing voice. For example, it is conceivable that a district with a strong desire to implement YRS might stack an advisory committee with members in favor of the new calendar. If the process is inequitable and unrepresentative, it may result in a decision to proceed that would be unlikely to build long-term support or commitment for the project. An unfairly constituted process that does not permit all perspectives to be heard cannot result in a valid determination of the appropriateness of the reform.

In one district we visited, educators from individual schools had indicated strong interest in proceeding with YRS but were not permitted to represent their perspectives on district-level committees. One school committee, made up of a principal, teachers, and parents, had been preparing for two years to obtain district permission to pilot YRS. The exclusion of those committee members from the district decision-making forum prevented them from having input into the process that might have enabled them to move ahead with implementation.

The most appropriate body for decision making about a calendar change is generally the group most likely to be directly affected by the implementation of the decision. For instance, having a district referendum on year-round schooling when only a couple of schools want to introduce a pilot project may prevent the experiment from being approved. Where people who are not directly affected by an impending calendar change are permitted to vote on a reform initiative, the outcome may be problematic. We have found that a reasonable threshold of support by those to be directly affected is the best indicator of whether to proceed with an innovation. In some instances, this has been set at approximately 60% of each separate constituent group: teachers, professional staff, and parents. In other instances, a collective threshold may be established.

Equity Considerations During Initiation

There are, however, some occasions when it may be more appropriate to make the decision to implement YRS on a district wide basis. Where this is the case, care must be taken to ensure that this is done equitably. In some districts we visited, policy had been instituted that provided guidelines requiring schools with enrollment levels above the school's designated capacity to implement multi-track schedules. In one such district, the policy was later undermined when individual schools were permitted to opt in or out on the basis of the political clout of the constituent parent group. This resulted in neighborhoods with less political influence having to follow district policy, while those with more power (and affluence) were permitted to circumvent it. Regardless of the level at which decisions are made, a school district has the obligation to develop and implement policy on an equitable basis.

An equitable decision-making process needs to include the following factors: a thorough and open investigation of the needs and concerns of the constituency, a discussion of the potential of the proposed reform to address them, and a match between the norms and beliefs of the constituents and the underlying assumptions of the proposal. Where this exploration occurs in an open and equitable process, permitting all positions to be heard, all questions asked, and all relevant information to be examined, we believe it will be successful.

In the foregoing discussion, we have indicated that in some districts, consultative processes were successful in disseminating accurate information, addressing concerns, and building support for an innovation. In others, we identified faulty processes related to the establishment of goals, communication, and representation.

We do not want to give the impression that any process of conceptualization or initiation that does not end in implementation of YRS is flawed or unsuccessful. Indeed, the opposite may well be the case. Following an initial exploration of YRS and a thorough exploration of the context, if it is determined that there is not a match, it would not only be inappropriate to proceed with implementation but important to avoid it.

Donato (1996) provided an excellent illustration of an inappropriate implementation decision that ignored the mismatch between the needs of one significant part of the community and program implementation. In a California community with a large population of migrant farm workers, the implementation of YRS in secondary schools resulted in a hardship when adolescents who were usually employed on the farms were required to attend school during the summer.

Policy Issues in the Initiation Phase

In many districts, much of the discussion concerning the possibility of a change to YRS hinges on the practices, contractual issues, and funding formulas in place at the time of the initial exploration. For example, a policy that requires districts to hire substitute teachers from an established "on-call list" would prevent teachers from being hired as substitutes during their off-track time, and hence constrain the flexibility of year-round schools. A collective agreement to limit the timing and length of faculty meetings (perhaps to one hour a week) may not work in a multi-track year-round school in which one longer meeting every three weeks on a track-change day might work better. One way to overcome difficulties may be to develop policies that emphasize *principles* rather than *existing practice*. For example, in the United States, the National Education Association's resolution F-11, reads, in part:

> Policies governing year-round schools must take into consideration the impact on the community and be in accordance with the Association's principles and professional salaries and class size. (National Educational Association, 1987, p. 18)

The emphasis on principles is useful because it allows for the possibility of change and provides a forum for discussion in which discourse may occur in a free and inclusive fashion. This approach allows resolution of issues and facilitates moving ahead to implement change while simultaneously protecting employees; insistence on the specifics of current practice sometimes stymies efforts to change. Where parties responsible for developing policy or for collective bargaining are willing to maintain the spirit of the law and to provide guidelines rather than restrictions, a change to YRS may be facilitated.

Summary of Initiation Concerns

A note of caution must be sounded. It is helpful to establish a climate in which an apocalyptic or cataclysmic attitude does not prevail. On the one hand, one sometimes hears statements to the effect that implementing year-round schooling will destroy the community and erode family values. On the other hand, there are arguments suggesting that, without multi-track year-round schooling, children will be forced into larger classes with split sessions, and their education will ultimately be jeopardized. These attitudes polarize thinking, reduce the inquiry to emotional levels, destroy credibility, and constrain the possibility of a fair and equitable outcome.

In all cases, the key is to obtain adequate commitment from those who will be involved with the early implementation of the new calendar without mandating a level of support that is unrealistic. Without this support, the next phase, *implementation*, is likely to be fraught with difficulties.

IMPLEMENTATION PHASE OF YRS

The *implementation* phase of a change process is sometimes considered to be primarily a technical stage in which policy simply needs to be enacted as conceived and adopted by a formal decision-making process. However, during *initiation and conceptualization*, an innovation is simply being considered. In the implementation phase, the concept needs to be lived. At this point, there is often the realization that ideas that seemed generally attractive and reasonable during an exploratory phase might require personal change, adaptation, and sometimes a lot of hard work. At times, this reality may be overwhelming and frightening. Thus, the highly political nature of the implementation phase may sometimes surprise those trying to introduce the reform in a technical way.

Implementing policy at a district level normally requires a series of legislative authorizations. The nature and extent of the requirements vary from jurisdiction to jurisdiction, but at a minimum, schools and districts must submit their proposed calendars for legislative approval by a designated date and show how the new calendar will maintain required instructional time. Some jurisdictions want a proposal that includes plans for staff development, student and parent orientation, communication to the wider community, and the evaluation of the innovation. In other areas the request also needs to demonstrate potential fiscal savings.

Communication During Implementation

Neither initial district consultations nor fulfillment of all of the legislative requirements necessarily ensures that people in local communities are aware that year-round schooling will be instituted in a way that will directly affect them. A local administrator, believing the decision has been well communicated and that everyone understands the implications, may begin to develop a new calendar and to distribute track request forms only to be deluged by outraged parents demanding an accounting. In one large district, we were told that the innovation had previously been widely disseminated, including a feature on a national television news program, but that when the time came for the year-round school calendar to be introduced into specific schools, parents came forward wondering what was being discussed and when the policy had been enacted.

Equity in Implementation

Although extensive and widespread early communication may reduce the political fallout during implementation, it would be naïve to expect it to eliminate political concerns altogether. In fact, every aspect of implementation is political. From the decision whether to implement single- or multi-track to offering intersession on a subsidized or cost-recovery basis; from the allocation of teachers and children to tracks and classrooms to the determination of bus routes; from the development of new contractual arrangements to the establishment of parent advisory councils under a year-round calendar—all have highly political overtones.

In each of these instances, the equity concerns we raised earlier come into play. Allocating children to classes needs to be done carefully to avoid ghettoizing any group of students on the tracks that appear the least desirable. Determining how resource teachers, music, and physical education specialists will provide for the needs of all students is also a highly sensitive issue. Placing all of a district's special programs for gifted students in traditional calendar schools and all of the resource or special needs programs in year-round schools also results in inequitable distribution of students and distorted perceptions of the schools. Sometimes, the need for multi-track schools arises in rapidly growing inner-city areas and results in a viewpoint that the calendar is only appropriate for schools in lower SES areas and not for upper-class suburban schools. Thus, equity concerns become part of every decision process.

Politicization of Implementation

Sometimes, politicization has negative effects on even a well-designed implementation. In one district, when a prominent superintendent's misconduct resulted in disfavor with the electorate, the whole year-round school innovation, with which he had been closely associated, was also discredited and ultimately discontinued. The strategic plan of another district was proceeding on schedule, with a number of schools having changed to a YR calendar. However, when it came time to institute year-round education in some of the more wealthy regions, parental outcry resulted in a reversal of the district policy.

Politicization is not always negative. It may raise the public awareness of an issue and bring it into the forum of public debate. In Donato's example (1996), although the Mexican-American community was not successful in achieving a reversal of the year-round school policy, it:

> came to understand that participation was a central part of the democratic formula, that this was a means to hold local educational institution[s] accountable and to integrate the Mexican American community into the decision-making process. (p. 192)

Thus, politicization may become a mechanism through which some previously disenfranchised people find voice and attain political power.

Role of the Media in Implementation

The role of the media must also be considered in implementation, for as soon as there is a hint of a controversial issue, reporters are present to exploit it. Again, this may have both positive and negative effects because the media can sway opinion in one direction or another. In one city, the disruptive presence of a vocal group of dissidents, Parents Against Multi-tracking (PAM), was widely reported in several newspapers. The district's decision to discontinue the exploration of YRS was largely attributed to their influence. Yet, only a few months later, a district representative reported that a public survey conducted by a local newspaper showed more than 70% of the public was supportive of the concept of YRS. This obvious contradiction demonstrates the disproportionate power that special interest groups can wield in decision-making processes.

In another instance, representatives from one district informed us that during the summer months, the media often called wanting student comments. During the time of the Mississippi flood, the media wanted to know if the school was engaged in any special relief projects. School officials indicated that the positive media attention during the summer was largely a result of their YR school being "the only game in town."

Summary of Implementation Issues

Recognition of the political nature of implementation may be critical to maintaining a focus and developing successful implementation strategies. If a district has originally introduced year-round schooling as a cost-saving measure, it should not feel it necessary to respond to political demands for proof that the innovation has resulted in improved student attendance, better test scores, or higher morale. Accountability and evaluation need to be consistent with the goals of the reform initiative.

The path from identifying needs within the educational context through the conceptualization and initiation phase to an adoption decision is just the beginning of the year-round school process. For the vision of year-round schooling to become a reality, it is necessary to attend to technical details and to political processes. Yet, despite the common practice of believing that the implementation of a successful program marks the end of the planning and political processes, the last stage recognized by many change theorists, that of *institutionalization and continuation* may, in fact, be the most difficult and challenging.

INSTITUTIONALIZATION AND CONTINUATION OF YRS

If an educational innovation is to become part of the culture of a school or district, then careful attention needs to be paid to what Fullan (1993) described as reculturing rather than simply restructuring. Restructuring is easy. Any legislative body may mandate a new structure such as a year-round school calendar or a new reporting system. However, we have been suggesting that if its success is to be more than temporary, a number of other issues need to be addressed simultaneously and on an ongoing basis.

Ongoing Evaluation and Assessment

In our opinion, one of the districts that has been the most success-ful at reculturing rather than simply restructuring is in Missouri. In this district, which has the distinction of having had the longest running multi-track year-round programs on the continent, year-round schooling was first implemented in 1969. At the end of the first year, a major outside funding agency conducted what turned out to be an inconclusive evaluation. Because both educators and the general public were aware that the analysis of test scores had not told an accurate or complete story, the district was not disheart-ened and continued to extend the year-round calendar into all of its elementary schools. The concept has now become so much a part of the culture of their elementary schools that educators there some-times talk about the year-round schedule as their "traditional cal-endar."

The issue of evaluation is more complex than it might appear at first glance. Although there is increasing and recent support in edu-cational research for the finding that year-round schools are often associated with improved academic achievement (Kneese, 1996; Shields & Oberg, 1999), the need of many districts to respond to a sometimes demanding and volatile political environment has re-sulted in some hasty and insubstantial studies. Motivated by po-litical demands to prove the success of their programs, some dis-tricts have attempted to show changes in academic achievement within the first couple of years of a new program. As might be ex-pected in the early stages of implementation, these results are of-ten inconclusive or even negative. Sometimes, year-round schools do not survive this initial disappointment of unchanged test scores. Ironically, this can happen even when districts do not set out to show an improvement in academic achievement but when the ini-tial goal has been to reduce the capital outlay.

At the opposite extreme of the investigation into the success or failure of year-round schooling is the phenomenon identified in several other districts. In these jurisdictions, rather than wanting to prove to an anxious public the efficacy of year-round schooling, district personnel are concerned with *not* demonstrating that one calendar is better in any way than another. One district contact person stated that in his experience, his district wanted an evaluation for any other new program after six months, but that even when year-round education had been in the district for 20 years, no one wanted to find out whether it made a difference. This respondent told us that, in his opinion, year-round school was "the best kept secret in the district." Elsewhere, we also found that district-level administrators were often reluctant to conduct evaluations that might set up a competitive situation within their district.

Our explanation for this phenomenon is that this respondent is right: districts generally do not want to know. If year-round schools are saving money but not performing adequately academically, then they would have to eliminate the year-round schools and find extra money. If, on the other hand, traditional schools are both less cost-effective and less successful academically, then a district might have to mandate that all schools move to a year-round schedule. In either case, the result of not knowing may be political peace. The cost of knowing may well be political upheaval.

Accountability

In view of the political difficulties of internal district evaluation, we believe that it is frequently useful for districts that have instituted alternative or modified calendars to work with a qualified outside researcher to assess the success of all of their structures and programs. Although feedback concerning the effects of an innovation should be ongoing from the outset, evaluators and their clients should be aware that summative evaluation should not be conducted until YRS has been in place for at least three years. Of necessity, a thorough evaluation will involve much more than test scores or tallies of general opinion polls. Responsible and accountable educational change requires understanding the ways in which any new program is or is not working and determining how it might be modified to function more effectively. Ethically and morally, when the public has been involved (or even when it has not) in the determination of a new educational direction, it has the right to know about the innovation's outcomes.

Sometimes promises are made during the implementation of YRS that are inappropriate. These may stem from the understandable enthusiasm that often accompanies new innovations. They may also come from an attempt to build support for the proposed calendar. Although it is important to have a clear direction in terms of what one hopes year-round schooling (or any other reform) may accomplish, global promises regarding outcomes (whether academic or fiscal) are generally inappropriate.

In one district, unfulfilled promises contributed to an ultimate inability to maintain year-round schooling. The district had promised that it would accompany the gradual phasing in of single-track year-round schooling with intersession activities to supplement the regular program. In each successive year of implementation the original intersession funding was cut back by 25%, until in the fourth year, it had been eliminated. We were told that the minute intersession funding hit zero, year-round schooling became much less attractive to parents, who then attacked the schedule. Moreover, constituents had been told that year-round schooling would result in better student achievement as measured by performance on standardized tests. When an evaluation of student achievement conducted in the first year showed no increase in test scores, disillusionment set in. The failure to fulfill these two promises resulted in a reversal of the district's plan to move all elementary schools to a form of year-round schooling.

In another district, where year-round schooling was mandated in three schools with little or no public consultation, few attempts were made to develop commitment or build support for the innovation. The patrons and personnel of these schools had been told that multi-track year-round school was a temporary solution to the pressures of overcrowding and that, if they were patient, a different (and presumably better) solution would soon be presented. The negativity associated with this approach was exacerbated by the introduction of several policies perceived to be unfair. District policy identified employees with a 240-day contract as 12-month employees and accorded them benefits commensurate with full-time status. With the implementation of multi-track year-round schooling, assistant principals and other extended contract employees were hired on 239-day contracts. This made these school-based educators ineligible for some benefits and vacation pay available for other full-time district employees. Five years later, personnel were still antagonistic toward the change, still waiting for it to disappear, and frustrated that the district had not only promised a temporary time frame to which it had failed to adhere but also that it had not made other adaptations that would have made YRS more attractive. Disappointment and a strong sense of betrayal occurred when there was little support for YRS and promises, both implicit and explicit, were not fulfilled.

Ongoing District Support

For institutionalization or continuation of year-round schooling to occur, it needs to be accompanied by ongoing district support, continued public awareness, and sustained commitment on the part of the leaders. If academic improvement is important, then support for programs associated with this goal needs to be maintained, and such innovations as intersession should receive predictable and continuous funding. If cost-effectiveness is important, then the analysis needs to take the combined operating and capital outlay costs into consideration. Frequent communication with the public will help to inform any newcomers to the community about the school calendar, to respond to any continuing concerns, and to permit modification of the calendar consistent with significant feedback that might be received.

District commitment is particularly important to the continuation of YRS. In several states, we found that once a group of schools had implemented the year-round calendar, then the district contact and support role was eliminated and the responsibility for year-round schooling was transferred to one of the local school principals. This placed a huge burden on the shoulders of these principals who were then responsible for ensuring that the rest of the district understood and responded to the needs of the existing year-round schools. The principals were also expected to respond to requests from outside visitors (school personnel and researchers) about year-round schooling in the district, a task that took countless hours. In several instances, we were told that in the absence of a district-level person who was responsible for year-round schooling, it would be extremely difficult for YRS to expand to other schools.

Summary of Continuation Issues

The political climate is, of course, a reality that can not only constrain but also promote the activities of any school district. If the potential for adverse political effects is to be overcome, leaders will need to ensure adequate time for consultation, communication, and committed support for the restructuring effort. In short, if year-round schooling is to become institutionalized as part of the culture of a district, all participants in the educational community need to work together to establish it as an ongoing means of offering education, rather than as a temporary solution to a problem.

CONCLUSION

The foregoing discussion emphasizes the political nature of the initiation, implementation, and continuation of year-round schooling. We have tried to suggest that where year-round schooling has been introduced as appropriate for the unique needs of a community and subsequently flounders, it is likely due to the failure of the implementers to recognize and work with the political processes rather than to any flaw inherent in the innovation itself. This is consistent with the perception of McDaniel (1993) who wrote:

> When confronted with significant change, many people will act with skepticism, resistance, and often outright hostility. This creates a significant political challenge for the school district and the community. This problem is exacerbated by the pervasive lack of attention to the political aspects of the move to year-round education on the part of school people. (p. 4)

McDaniel suggests that the change to year-round schooling needs to be approached as a political campaign. We agree that there is considerable strategy involved in any change effort; however, we have emphasized the need for a collaborative process that overcomes the concept of winners and losers.

In some instances, the way year-round schooling has been set up has almost ensured its eventual failure. Anyone wanting to avoid the pitfalls will have to take the dynamics of change into consideration. Among the characteristics identified by Hargreaves and Fullan (1998) for successful educational change are greater flexibility, increased interaction between a school and its environment, identification of an educational moral purpose, a recognition of the emotional aspects of change, and capacity building, "which focuses on the motivation, skill and resources that are needed to perform at a high level" (p. 72). They suggest that "effective educational change always needs a blend of pressure and support but most [governing bodies] have exerted far too much pressure . . . and provided not nearly enough capacity building and support" (p. 72-73).

There is no template for educational change and definitely no single correct way to introduce year-round schooling. Nevertheless, we suggest that any district wanting to implement a calendar change will have to carefully consider whether the selected calendar meets the needs of the local area. Underestimating the force of the political factors will lead to eventual failure. On the other hand, educational political awareness requires that policy makers at all levels remain sensitive to local pressures, challenges, and realities.

CHAPTER 10:

FISCAL CONSIDERATIONS AND

YEAR-ROUND SCHOOLING

Economic considerations, even with double-digit mill-rate increases to meet the high and rising educational costs, do not have the persuasive power to foster exploration of the savings to be gained by alternative scheduling. (Perry, 1991, p. 15)

*****

One rationale for going to a balanced multi-track calendar was that we could cut down by 12 relocatables. That's a $60,000 per classroom savings. That's 12 classrooms times $60,000. It's an economic issue. (District representative)

*****

There is little doubt that economic issues constitute one of the dominant reasons why schools and districts first begin to explore the possibility of year-round schooling. However, there is little agreement, either in the YRS literature or among districts, about how to assess the fiscal impact or about the actual cost savings that may be achieved. These difficulties are compounded because the operating costs and capital outlays are frequently confused. The latter refer to all monies expended to provide facilities for the educational activities of a district, including acquisition of the land and erection of buildings. Operating costs refer to the annual expenditures required to offer the educational programs in the district and include items such as utility costs, bussing, educational materials, and salaries. To add to the confusion, fiscal issues also become confounded with educational concerns. Not suprisingly, there are economic con-

FISCAL CONSIDERATIONS AND YRS

siderations related to single-track year-round schooling as well as pedagogical implications for multi-track models. This chapter explores these complex issues.

Year-round schooling is not the only method districts use to save money and to house students in times of rapid growth and overcrowded schools. O'Neil and Adamson (1993) explain that while their district uses multi-track year-round schooling for its most overcrowded elementary schools, it also utilizes other strategies to alleviate overcrowding. For instance, they describe some creative staffing patterns including hiring aides to assist teachers in overcrowded schools, permitting secondary school teachers to voluntarily teach during their prep periods, making use of split classes or multi-age, cross-grade groupings, and instituting magnet programs and open enrollment. They also make use of portable classrooms, divide large classrooms to make space for two smaller units, add modular wings to existing schools, and create satellite buildings. Other adaptations frequently mentioned in other districts include the use of extended and overlapping or split shift schedules.

There are generally social costs as well as increased operating costs associated with most of these options. Portable classrooms usually have poorer construction, less insulation, and sometimes require additional washrooms, air-conditioning, or intercom systems. Many of the other arrangements, such as split shifts or extended day, while not requiring additional expenditures, are considered to be unpopular stopgap measures. The initial capital outlay for modular and relocatable wings or portable classrooms may be lower than for new school construction. Thus, although they add considerably to the costs of a school or district, they are generally thought to be insignificant and relatively temporary solutions. There is rarely much public discussion, debate, or consultation due to the incremental nature of most of these changes. Few schools set out, for example, to have 15 or 20 portable classrooms on their grounds but gain them a few at a time.

Year-round schooling, on the other hand, is seen as a significant and more permanent change. For that reason, there is often a great amount of discussion about the potential costs and benefits of year-round schooling. We briefly discuss some of the literature related to fiscal issues and YRS and then turn to a discussion of the cost frameworks and analytical categories for understanding the attendant fiscal issues.

FROM THE LITERATURE

In general, the YRS literature related to fiscal issues falls into three main categories. Most overviews of YRS make casual mention of the costs and benefits. Many school and district analyses deal with savings or costs accrued, often early in the implementation of YRS, although many of these are not published but available only through the individual districts. A third group presents analytical costing frameworks to help people determine the fiscal viability of the innovation. In general, overviews of YRS mention its potential for savings due to avoidance of capital costs required for the construction of new buildings. Some of the literature fails to differentiate between fiscal issues related to single and multi-track YRS. This results in confusion when one seeks findings related to a specific year-round school calendar.

There is no consensus in the literature about whether YRS saves money. Denton and Walenta (1993) cite the example of a district in California and say that when the district factored in the capital costs it would have expended for new buildings, it found that YRS does save money. Goren and Carriedo (1986) identify increased costs largely due to inclusion of transitional expenses such as new district forms, increased rubbish disposal, and new vehicles required by the transportation department. Some of the literature indicates that year-round schooling costs more than its traditional counterpart, primarily because there is confusion between capital and operational costs.

Although most of the studies suggest that YRS are more expensive to operate than traditional-calendar schools (TCS), White (1992) identified the unanticipated costs when Jefferson County, Colorado, after 14 years on a MT year-round calendar, returned to a traditional calendar. He clarified the need to distinguish between the costs for an individual school and those that are district expenditures by saying, "even though each school's total operating costs rise when the school switches to a year-round schedule, the district's unit costs drop" (p. 30). He added,

When Jefferson County built and opened new schools to displace the year-round operation, the district's total operating costs far exceeded the costs for serving the same enrollment on a year-round calendar. Yet no one had ever made a convincing case to the public that explained the savings involved in the year-round approach." (p. 30)

While there are numerous district studies in which there is detailed analysis of parent, student, and teacher satisfaction, few assess the costs or fiscal benefits of year-round schooling. This is particularly interesting in view of one of the primary stated purposes: to save money. Brekke (1983, 1985) presented extensive cost analyses of YRS in Oxnard School District. In each analysis, the general findings were similar, that "YRE within the Oxnard School District has shown a very substantial saving in operational and capital expense . . . [It] has, in the absence of school building funds, kept the District from a massive program of double/half-day session classes" (1985, p. 16).

COSTING CATEGORIES

In 1983, Levin suggested that costing frameworks be based on commonly used categories sometimes called *ingredients*. This *ingredients method* has been taken up by a number of writers. In this method, the most commonly used categories are "capital, operational, transition cost calculations, and incentive revenues" (Zykowski et al., 1991, p. 26). Quinlan and associates (1987) added the category of "incidental differences" to represent the impact on revenues of changed attendance, vandalism, or discipline. From these frameworks, we will use the five categories of *capital costs, operating costs, transitional costs, special funding and incentives*, and *incidental differences* to discuss some issues related to the funding of YRS. The components of these ingredients are discussed below.

Capital Costs

Some authors (Quinlan et al., 1987; Zykowski et al., 1991), also use the term *avoided costs* to refer to capital outlay that a district may keep from spending if it is able to successfully implement some form of efficiency calendar such as year-round school. One of the primary reasons for instituting multi-track calendars is to accommodate more students in existing buildings and, hence, avoid or postpone the necessity of new school construction. In fact, significant space advantages are associated with many of the most common MT models of year-round schooling. Appendix A illustrates the potential space savings of various calendars in more detail. It shows that, depending on the approach chosen, from 25–50% more students may be housed with no additional space needed. A five-track system, sometimes called a *quinmester*, in which students attend four of the five terms, offers a 25% saving. In the 45-15 calendar, four tracks rotate in sequence with three present at any one time and one on vacation. This permits 33% more students to be housed in the existing building. Less common plans like the three-track Concept 6 use a shorter number of days per student but extend the length of the school day. With two of the three tracks present at any one time, the school is able to accommodate 50% more students.

Sometimes capital expenditures are included in the cost-benefit analysis of YRS; sometimes they are excluded. It is essential to consider them in the overall fiscal analysis of YRS, because the avoidance of new construction accounts for most of the cost savings over time. These costs, however, vary substantially with local conditions: availability of land, building costs, and the amount of infrastructure required (streets, sewer, water, and electrical).

One of the relevant local conditions is the number of portable classrooms that may be erected for an existing building before new construction is required. This, too, depends on several factors, such as space and land constraints, district policy and local codes, and the capacity of the school core. The core, representing the common facilities such as restrooms, auditoriums, administrative offices, libraries, and gymnasiums, is only able to support a finite number of students at any one time, whether in regular classrooms or portables. When it reaches its saturation point, either a new building or a changed schedule is needed. Thus, the cost of portable classrooms, although considerably less than building new schools, is a capital cost that needs to be factored in to the cost-benefit calculation.

A simple example of a capital cost calculation may help. If the normal capacity of elementary schools within a district on a traditional calendar is 600 students, and the district enrollment grows by 600 students, then one way to handle the growth would be to build a new school. If the per pupil cost of a new school, including building and site were estimated at approximately $15,000 per student, then the total cost of the school would be $9 million. Another way to accommodate the same 600 students would be to place them in several schools, for example, four schools at 150 additional students each, on a multi-track year-round schedule. Although the total operating costs for each of these schools would increase on the basis of their new and higher enrollment, a true baseline for comparisons would include the potential capital cost of building, equipping, and staffing a new school for the same number of students.

Operating Costs

There is little difference between the operating costs of a single-track year-round school and a traditional-calendar school unless the calendar change has been accompanied by additional voluntary programs or building modifications. Our discussion of operating costs focuses primarily on the expenses associated with multi-track year-round schools. Some authors (Quinlan et. al., 1987; Denton & Walenta, 1993) attempt to divide these operating costs into two categories: fixed and variable; however, there is much confusion about what is fixed (independent of the student population being served) and what is variable (costs experienced on a per student basis). For example, utility costs may be fixed or variable depending on whether the average costs per week remain relatively constant regardless of the calendar or whether extra operating costs are seen to relate directly to the additional student time in a building. Because this is so difficult to determine with accuracy, we suggest that the distinction between fixed and variable costs is not particularly useful. What is appropriate, as previously suggested, is to separate the costs of what is needed to operate schools on a year-round calendar and those additional provisions that may have been selected to enhance the year-round schedule. Only the former should be included in any cost comparison calculations.

Among the operating costs that need to be considered are items such as administrative and teacher salaries, bussing and transportation, program costs, instructional materials, and school maintenance. In each case, many of these costs would be incurred whether or not a school was on a year-round schedule. However, the increased total student body will certainly result in some additional expenditure. Of necessity, transportation costs change when student numbers increase. Additional students require additional teachers and often, supplementary programs. Maintenance costs for a MT year-round school, such as deep cleaning on a more regular basis, will also increase due to the extended operating time and the increased capacity. An additional expenditure may be needed for textbooks although there are two common ways for multi-track schools to provide textbooks for students: allocation by pupil or by desk. If a school chooses to assign books by desk, there will be no need to purchase new texts to accommodate more students, although there will be increased loss and additional wear and tear. Many multi-track year-round schools also qualify for some additional administrative and support staff due to their increased size. However, it is necessary that fiscal calculations include a comparison of the costs of adding a vice-principal, part-time assistant principal, or clerical staff in expansion schools with the price of a full complement of administrative and office staff should a new building be opened.

It is important to note that sometimes district policy may affect the operational costs of a year-round school. For instance, frequently certified teachers are permitted to act as substitute teachers during their off-track periods. If they are hired at a substitute rate of pay, then there will be no fiscal impact on the school. But if, as in some places, they are hired at their regular daily rate of pay, then there will be increased costs to the school's substitute budget. Although our emphasis is on the fiscal issues, it is important to note that paying more to have teachers who are familiar with the children and the school is probably, in the long run, an effective and efficient use of funds.

Another policy that has the potential to affect the operational costs of a year-round school relates to the allocation of teachers and classes to tracks. If the tracks are balanced so that the school operates at relatively full capacity on each track, the economies of scale are maximized. In some districts, in which there is a policy to grant parental track requests rather than to balance tracks, schools are sometimes placed in the position of needing to retain portables in order to accommodate the tracks with the heaviest request levels. This, of course, reduces the fiscal benefits that may be accrued through multi-track scheduling, while also exacerbating scheduling and management problems.

It is clear from the foregoing discussion, which has focused primarily on multi-track year-round schooling, that the operating costs will increase when the student population is augmented in a particular school. The most valid comparison is a per pupil one that takes into account the proportional increase of the student body and compares the relative costs to others throughout a district. We would go so far as to say that, if there is not some increased expenditure at the individual school level, savings might have been realized at the expense of the students' education. In addition, in the early stages of the change from a traditional to year-round calendar school, there are some one-time costs that may be more accurately termed transitional costs.

Transitional Costs

Transitional costs are those related to the change from a traditional calendar schedule to a year-round schedule and thus are not recurring. They are, in some ways, similar to the costs of moving and installing portable classrooms.

There are two basic categories of transitional costs: those related to preparing for and planning the implementation of YRS and those required to enable an existing facility to accommodate the YR schedule. In the first category are all of the costs of investigating the appropriateness of year-round schooling, including hiring consultants and outside facilitators, conducting feasibility studies and literature searches, printing brochures and information packages, and engaging in public hearings and consultations. Another large part of the preparation expenses includes pre-service training and planning time for administrators and, to a lesser extent, the teachers.

A second category of transitional expenses concerns readying the facility. Minimal but critical expenditures in this category include providing for the storage of teachers' supplies and materials, and sometimes student materials as well, while they are off-track. The most common strategy to accommodate off-track storage is the construction of large movable cabinets in which teachers may store their materials and supplies. Other facility changes may, but do not necessarily, include changes to teacher work areas, exterior signs to announce track changes, and modifications to common use areas.

Perhaps the major expenditure required to prepare many facilities is air-conditioning. This cost needs to be carefully considered because of the complexity of the situation. Although the installation of air-conditioning is a one-time expense, its benefits continue over quite a few years. Thus, although air-conditioning may rightly be considered a transitional expense, to make cost comparisons, the equipment and installation costs should be amortized over a period of years. In addition, the continuing expense of operating the air-conditioning system should be included in the calculation of operating costs.

At times, the difficulty of equipping an older building with air-conditioning may be so costly that it may not be feasible to institute YRS in that building. The costs need to be weighed carefully against the projected length of time that a particular school is anticipated to experience overcrowding. Although air-conditioning is mentioned frequently in the literature as a requirement of YRS, it is only necessary where the temperatures during the months of extended operation regularly and significantly exceed those of the traditional calendar schools in the same district. For instance, while summer months in the northern states or Canada may be hot, the temperatures may still be lower than in many other areas where traditional-calendar schools operate without air-conditioning on a regular basis. Some other requested transitional costs may also be unnecessary.

Special Funding and Incentives

Special funding and incentive revenues may fall into several categories: incentives specifically intended to promote cost-saving approaches such as year-round schooling or grants offered to special programs assigned to YRS that help to defray some of the expenditures. Sometimes jurisdictions offer financial incentives to schools that move to year-round calendars. For example, California at one time offered a per pupil bonus in excess of $125 for each pupil placed in a year-round school for the purpose of saving space and money. Other jurisdictions offer de facto incentives for year-round schooling by allocating funds for new school construction only to districts that agree that their new schools will be on year-round schedules. Elsewhere, the distribution of funds for new schools is restricted by imposing a mandate for districts to be "more efficient" in their use of space. Although in many districts this leads to YRS as the alternative of choice, the innovation is not specified in the funding mandate.

At other times, a district may make incentive funding available to specific schools that choose to change to a year-round schedule. Frequently, these incentives are offered to individual schools in the form of additional equipment such as computer labs or music programs. Occasionally, small financial incentives are provided to teachers and administrators on a year-round schedule. Such provisions are highly idiosyncratic. While they are offered by some districts, many make no special concessions to personnel in year-round schooling. Some incentives we have found included a $25 stipend to teachers for track-change days (to compensate for needing to pack and move materials) and $1,000 administrative bonuses to YRS principals.

Other allocations also fall into the category of special funds. These monies, which come primarily from outside agencies or federal programs, are often targeted for specific populations that occur with more frequency in many year-round schools. Such costs need to be carefully disentangled and reported accurately when fiscal comparisons are made.

Because overcrowding tends to occur in rapidly growing areas with high proportions of at-risk students, some YRS programs are often funded, in part, through government assistance. Thus, although a new breakfast program may coincide with the institution of the year-round calendar, if it is funded outside of regular school district funds, its cost should not be included in the YRS fiscal considerations. Similarly, a number of poorly performing schools in urban areas have begun to offer year-round school and intersession programs in an attempt to rehabilitate the school's academic reputation. If funds for remedial programs would have been available, regardless of the calendar change, they too should be excluded from the calculations.

Incidental Differences

The final category, incidental differences, is not always included in costing frameworks, although it has the potential to significantly alter the findings. It is different in nature from the others because these differences cannot be estimated prior to the implementation of YRS. These incidental differences relate to some unanticipated savings that accrue as a result of better teacher and student attendance, lower vandalism rates, fewer disciplinary incidents, and increased community recreational opportunities. Each of these factors has been identified as a frequent and unanticipated benefit of implementing year-round school calendars. Each may bring attendant fiscal savings to a school or district. For example, in one elementary school that had recently instituted a dual-calendar approach, we were informed that teacher attendance had improved markedly and that associated substitute teacher costs had decreased by thousands of dollars during the first year. We were then surprised to learn that in a neighboring school, YRS had not had a positive impact on teacher attendance or substitute budgets. When we asked for some elaboration, we were told that the school had traditionally had one of the highest rates of teacher attendance in the area and, thus, had little or no room for improvement.

Although we have also reported that many year-round schools experienced a decrease in student disciplinary incidents and vandalism rates, some schools identified no difference in these dimensions. We have also found that, perhaps due to the improved communication between YRS and their communities, the implementation of YRS often acted as a catalyst for a new relationship that was mutually beneficial. Sometimes the community recreation program was permitted to use school facilities for training and activities and, in turn, began to offer more of these activities in three-week clusters so students off-track might take advantage of them.

Summary of Costs

In this section, we have provided an overview of five categories that need to be included in a cost analysis of year-round schooling: *capital costs, operating costs, transitional costs, special funding and incentives,* and *incidental differences.* In the next section we discuss the advantages and disadvantages of three of the most commonly proposed frameworks for the analysis of these ingredients.

FRAMEWORKS FOR THE FISCAL ANALYSIS OF YEAR-ROUND SCHOOLING

Several writers (Baker et al., 1978; Hazelton et al., 1992; Hough et al., 1990; Zykowski et al., 1991) describe three primary methods for analyzing school calendars, particularly for comparing the respective costs and benefits of year-round schooling with those of traditional calendar schools. The first method often suggested is the *single-school comparative method*. This method compares a school's budget under a year-round calendar with the budget of the same school for prior years under the traditional schedule. The second, the *matched-school comparative method*, is the comparison of the budget for a year-round school with that of a matched traditional calendar school in the same year. Third, is the *simulated comparative method*. This involves a comparison of the budget for a year-round school with a simulation of what it would cost if the school, in the same year, were running under a traditional calendar. Each of the methods has particular advantages and disadvantages.

Single-School Comparative Method

The single-school comparative method compares a YRS budget with its own prior traditional-calendar budget. Although the data are readily available from existing reports, this is not a true comparison for two main reasons. The first is that there is a maturation or inflation effect. Schools are not static but change from year to year. For example, a set of textbooks may be purchased in one year and will not need replacement for several more years. Returning teachers often automatically move higher on a salary grid, increasing the payroll costs for the school. Costs of heating, electricity, and other services are also subject to economic inflation. The budget for a given year is almost always higher than for the previous year. A valid comparison would have to allow for inflation and factor out costs that would have increased even if the calendar had not changed.

The second difficulty with the single-school comparative method is that a calendar change is almost always accompanied by other educational innovations. As Baker and others (1978) said, "The change from a YRS schedule seems to act as a catalyst for a variety of innovations, some of which are facilitated by the YRS schedule but are almost never inherent in the YRS schedule" (p. 222). During the decision to adopt a new calendar, the frequent consultations with the community may result in the school's establishment of special programs to better meet the community's needs. Some

examples of these may be daycare programs, after-school enrichment activities, and new instructional initiatives. In several schools
we studied, educational programs for parents, family activities, special newsletters, and additional educational materials accompanied
the institution of year-round calendars. There is no reason why a
traditional calendar school could not implement similar programs.
Because most of these changes are not intrinsic to YRS, it would not
be appropriate to attribute their budgetary impact to the calendar
change. These new programs should, therefore, be excluded from
any cost comparison.

Even when there is no direct counterpart to a traditional-calendar program, some special programs such as YRS intersession
should not be included in the cost analysis. There are two reasons
for this exclusion. First, intersession is not a mandatory or intrinsic part of year-round schooling, despite its beneficial and desirable
attributes. Second, funding for intersession programs may come
from a variety of sources, such as a district's reallocation of summer school budgets, special grants, social services subsidies, or
parental user fees.

Matched-School Comparative Method

Comparing a YRS with a matched traditional-calendar school has
the advantage of using available information from the same year.
Although it can avoid errors attributable to inflation, it is extremely
difficult to achieve proper matching or to correct, statistically, for
any mismatches. Some of the factors that need to be considered but
that are extremely difficult to match are: facility costs, including
utilities and maintenance; community factors, such as bus routes
and size of catchment area; program costs, including class size,
special education, and remedial and enrichment activities; and the
formidable category of personnel costs. The latter are based on negotiated salaries and experience increments as well as changing
formulas for ratios of teachers, aides, and office personnel. Moreover, matching schools requires consideration of student, staff, and
community characteristics such as socioeconomic status (SES).

As for the previous method, another difficulty of using budgets
for cost comparisons is that existing budget categories do not necessarily include all relevant factors broken out so they may be

clearly identified. Some programs may be partially funded by other sources, costs of one program may be embedded within another, and budgets are sometimes as much guidelines for expenditures as actual accountings of how money was spent.

Simulated Comparative Method

Because of the previously identified difficulties with comparative analyses, a third model, using a simulated analysis, was developed in 1978 by Baker, Pelavin, and Burnett. This model was subsequently elaborated and refined by Hough and colleagues in 1990. The simulation model involves creating a detailed accounting of the costs of an educational program on a YR calendar and then estimating, or simulating, what it would cost to operate an identical program on a traditional calendar in the same year in the same building.

To effect an acceptable comparison, it is necessary to calculate the costs on a long-term basis (perhaps 20 years) and to project the simulation over the same period of time. The calendar has to be the sole independent variable, with the educational programs consistent, the building capacity stable, and the assumed average daily attendance held constant.

This model requires substantial work to prepare the figures. Nevertheless, many suggest that the increased accuracy more than compensates for the complexity of the approach. Some writers (Richmond, 1978), however, provide the critique that a simulation is not a replication and that it rarely takes all relevant contextual factors into consideration.

Summary

Regardless of the model chosen, it is important to identify the basis of the comparison being used. Comparisons of operating costs may be made at either the individual school or the district level. However, when capital outlay is included, the district is the only viable unit of analysis. When extraneous characteristics are factored out, costs per pupil for single-track schools are likely to be similar to those for traditional calendar schools. School-level costs of multi-track schools will, of course, be higher than for the same school on a traditional calendar because of the increased capacity. Thus, comparison on a school wide basis is less valid than a per pupil cost analysis across the district.

CONCLUSION

The discussion of costing frameworks has suggested that the issue of determining the costs or benefits of a change to either single- or multi-track year-round schooling is remarkably complex and difficult. There is no one right method or exact formula that may be adopted. The *single-school comparative method* seems to be the best way to identify the incidental costs or benefits of a calendar change. The *matched-school comparison* may well work best for an analysis of per pupil operating costs, if one is careful to achieve an appropriate match and to factor out relevant differences. The need to amortize capital costs and some transitional costs (air-conditioning) over a multi-year period suggests that a *simulation method* may be the most appropriate for these categories of costs or savings. When special revenues and incentives need to be identified, none of the accepted methods is entirely adequate for the analysis, because these moneys are not necessarily inherent in the change to year-round schooling but are associated with specific school and community characteristics.

It may be helpful to use the following equation (similar to the one used by Hough et al., 1990) to represent a formula for a cost-benefit analysis.

CAPITAL (costs or savings) + OPERATIONAL (costs or savings)
+ TRANSITIONAL (costs or savings)
+ SPECIAL FUNDING (grants and incentives)
+ INCIDENTAL (costs or savings)

= TOTAL (costs or savings)

It is then possible to divide the total by the number of enrolled students to attain a per-pupil cost or saving to the district.

TOTAL ÷ NUMBER OF ENROLLED PUPILS

= PER PUPIL (costs or savings).

Although there is no single correct way to develop a satisfactory cost-benefit analysis of a calendar change to year-round schooling, there are some clear guidelines that emerge from this discussion. Modifications that are necessarily part of the calendar change to either single- or multi-track year-round school should be included, whereas those that are accompanying but not inherent alterations should be excluded. This is not to suggest a district examining the overall costs of its programs should not consider them, but that they are not relevant to a comparison of the costs of YRS and TCS. Operating costs of a multi-track year-round school will be higher than for the same school on a traditional calendar, but when per pupil costs, over time, are considered, a more accurate picture emerges; therefore, capital costs and operating expenses must be considered together for an accurate analysis to occur.

Clear identification of the calendar being discussed, careful delineation of costs and savings, and judicious guidelines for what is included or excluded from the calculation will provide an accurate and accountable assessment of the fiscal implications of a change to year-round schooling.

CONCLUSION

Looked at rationally and dispassionately, year-round education is too good to pass up. How many educational innovations can boast that they improve instruction, offer lifestyle advantages to families and staffs, and save millions of dollars? (McDaniel, 1993, p.4)

*****

For most of a century, North Americans have equated the September Labor Day holiday with the end of summer vacation and the beginning of a new school year. It is not surprising that this traditional school calendar has become entrenched as a cultural icon, as universally accepted as the traditional celebrations of the Christmas season or Thanksgiving. Community organizations, travel groups, and businesses have capitalized on the long summer break to offer recreational activities and sports leagues for children, promote vacation tour packages, and advertise extensive back-to school sales. Often, the general public has envied (and sometimes criticized) teachers for their shortened work year and long summer vacations.

It is little wonder that when a calendar change to YRS is presented as a new concept in any district, it is frequently accompanied by mixed emotions: anticipation, anxiety, angst, and sometimes, strong resistance. Because school calendars could be considered paradigms, the new way of thinking required to implement a form of YRS, might be called a *paradigm shift*.

YEAR-ROUND SCHOOLING: A PARADIGM SHIFT

In 1962, Thomas Kuhn presented his theory about paradigm shifts in his now famous treatise, *The Structure of Scientific Revolutions*. The Oxford Dictionary defines a *paradigm* as an "example or model of how things should be done." The term encompasses all of the understandings and expectations commonly held by a particular culture or community about a given phenomenon. Before Copernicus, for example, the common Western European understanding was of a geocentric universe. This paradigm was one in which the earth stood at the center of the universe while the rest of the planets and stars revolved around it. It was only after considerable struggle that the Copernican theory was accepted and people began to embrace the new paradigm and view the earth and heavens in different ways. This change in understanding is an example of what Kuhn refers to as a paradigm shift.

Kuhn (1970), noting that one characteristic of a paradigm shift was often strong initial resistance to a new idea, stated "history suggests that the road to a firm research consensus is extraordinarily arduous" (p. 15). We do not suggest that a change to year-round schooling constitutes a shift in understanding in any way similar in magnitude to the acceptance of a heliocentric solar system. However, it seems that society's reluctance to change the traditional school calendar is consistent with Kuhn's explanation of a paradigm shift. This may also help to explain why the research community seems to be having difficulty in reaching consensus about YRS.

It is clear that not everyone would agree, as McDaniel (1993) suggested, that year-round schooling is always "too good to pass up." In fact, YRS is sometimes introduced in such a way as to have a negative impact on the morale of teachers and the wider community. Yet, if it is chosen appropriately and implemented with care, we believe in its potential to provide the benefits mentioned in the quotation that opened this chapter.

Frequently, the landscape of YRS is a confused jumble of facts and opinions, conflicting perceptions and claims, supported by uneven research and provocative polemic. Again, this is consistent with how Kuhn (1970) described the emergence of a new paradigm in which "early fact gathering is a far more random activity than subsequent research activity" (p. 17). The interpretation of new facts, Kuhn recognized, requires at least an "implicit body of intertwined theoretical and methodological belief that permits selection, evaluation, and criticism" (p. 17).

WHAT DOES YEAR-ROUND SCHOOLING HAVE TO DO WITH EDUCATION?

In the previous chapters, we have presented some ideas, facts, and perceptions intended to help sort through the myriad of promises and critiques of year-round schooling and to assist with the investigation of a model that may be appropriate for a given school or community. In this chapter we want to bring together some issues and ideas related, not only to school-calendar change, but to educational reform in general. If a move to YRS is considered to be simply a structural change in the dates of school terms and vacations, it is unlikely that year-round schooling will have much to do with education. However, if the calendar change is considered in relation to other conceptual—structural, cultural, and pedagogical— aspects of schooling, we believe it may have everything to do with education. We argue, not for a separate consideration of stakeholder perspectives or discrete advantages or disadvantages of YRS, but for a holistic examination of how a calendar change may have a more significant impact on the teaching and learning environment of the school.

To pull these ideas together in a useful and concise way, we first present a matrix that demonstrates how the theoretical and methodological issues, previously discussed as separate topics, may be intertwined in a conceptual approach to examining year-round schooling. In the next part of the chapter we consider some additional factors related to implementing school reform: assessment and evaluation, the change process itself, and educational leadership. Finally, we offer some more personal reflections on the potential of YRS to positively affect the education of children and youth.

A CONCEPTUAL MATRIX FOR EXAMINING YEAR-ROUND SCHOOLING

The following matrix is intended to provide an overview of many of the components of effective educational change. It affords a unified though simplistic representation of elements that are too often considered separately, but that are all essential components of a thorough consideration of year-round schooling (or any other educational reform initiative). It is useful as a heuristic device for understanding the complexity of the issues involved in the consideration, adoption, and implementation of year-round schooling.

The vertical axis of Figure 11.1 contains three criteria for considering educational change: *responsibility, equity,* and *sustainability.* On the horizontal axis are four domains of schooling: the *political, social, fiscal,* and *educational.* We believe each domain should be considered with each of the three criteria to help educators to assess the appropriateness of any educational reform. In the following section, we discuss the matrix using the headings of the three criteria we have selected.

A note of caution should be sounded here. We are not generally fond of organizing ideas into a diagram or matrix for a number of reasons. First, a matrix tends to simplify and perhaps compartmentalize what are usually very complex and integrated concepts. Second, it frequently implies that a selection may be made from among elements in different parts of a matrix. Finally, it suggests that all relevant ideas may be summed up in a relatively simple and concrete way. None of these is suggested by our schematic for considering a change to year-round schooling. Rather, we emphasize again the need to consider the matrix holistically.

Figure 11.1 A conceptual model for consideration of YRS.

	Political	Social	Fiscal	Educational
Responsible	Legitimacy of interest, degree of influence	Consider various interests	Comprehensive, holistic, integrated	No detrimental effects, enhance opportunities
Equitable	Access for all groups	Integration rather than separation	Use $$ to reduce inequities	Improve experiences of those most in need
Sustainable	Plan for a long-term rather than temporary solution	Adapt to social and cultural conditions	Allocate adequate $$ to support the innovation	Ensure opportunities for renewal

Making YRS a Responsible Change

Responsibility, as we have conceptualized it, includes accountability to all groups that have a stake in an innovation. A structural or organizational change to an institution such as public education does not only affect those who work or study within a school, but the wider community as well. If YRS is *politically responsible*, it will be implemented with due regard for democratic processes. There will be sufficient public consultation, access to policy makers by those with a legitimate interest in the innovation, and open and thorough decision-making processes. Mark and Shotland (1985) suggest legitimacy of interest and degree of influence as criteria for helping to decide who should actually participate in a decision-making process. Educational decisions are somewhat different from other types of political decisions because society as a whole is perceived to have a legitimate interest in seeing that everyone becomes well educated. Nevertheless, not all citizens have the same degree of legitimacy of interest and, therefore, should not be accorded equally strong voices in the process. For example, a classroom teacher or a family with children in a given school have strong legitimate interests and should also have a high degree of influence in a proposal to change the school calendar. On the other hand, a private summer camp director wanting to attract clients or the supervisor of a university teacher education program wanting a convenient schedule for the placement of student teachers have weaker and less direct interests and should not have the same degree of influence.

We have suggested elsewhere that sometimes the decision-making process is co-opted by those who have loud voices but a less legitimate stake in the outcomes. It is important to ensure that where implementation will affect only a small group of parents, or a few specific schools, the voices of their representatives be given the greatest influence. This would prevent those with political power but little legitimate interest in the change from opposing either implementation or continuation of an innovation. As an illustration, we recall the situation of several districts in which the opinions of people already piloting the year-round calendar were virtually ignored. In each case, at a public meeting of the elected school board, a vote was called before granting permission to those who were already involved in YRS to address the meeting. In contrast, the decision of several other districts to permit local communities to select their own calendars seems to be a more effective approach.

A *socially responsible* process will also ensure that the various needs of different community groups are considered in order that constituents perceive their needs have been both heard and understood. This does not mean, of course, that any decision will please everyone involved or that every group will believe that the final decision is positive. It does require that the processes of consultation include the full range of stakeholder interests, some of which may not always be included in a purely political process. Among these might be parent councils, community recreation leagues, and representatives of local businesses who often have a need for information concerning a proposed change.

A *fiscally responsible* reform takes a comprehensive, integrated, and holistic approach to determine fiscal costs and benefits. We have discussed the importance of considering long-term capital costs and savings as well as transitional expenses and ongoing operating costs in any determination of financial advantages or disadvantages. Although fiscal responsibility sometimes requires additional expenditures to be used as incentives to implement a reform, this does not justify large-scale expenditures where they may not be warranted. A prerequisite for schools to be air-conditioned before moving to a year-round schedule may be essential in the southern states but unnecessary in parts of Canada. Likewise, providing a small bonus to year-round school administrators working additional time, or to teachers required to change classrooms regularly on a multi-track schedule, may be desirable. Irresponsible decisions do not take the human factor into consideration, whereas responsible decisions include a recognition that when people take on greater responsibility, they should generally be compensated for it and their contracts changed to reflect new and perhaps more comprehensive duties.

Responsible decisions require that the educational needs of a community be considered. In our matrix, the heading *educational* refers to the broad processes of learning in academic, social, and cultural ways and includes both personal and collective domains. For a decision to implement year-round schooling to be *educationally responsible*, the academic issues need to be considered in conjunction with the fiscal, social, and political components. An implementation decision seen solely (or even primarily) as a cost-saving measure, without discussion of the attendant educational issues, is unlikely to succeed. The most educationally accountable year-round programs we have described have been planned to ensure that the educational benefits of the calendar change (regardless of the initial impetus for the change) were foremost in ongoing discussions. Examples of educational considerations include a decision to allocate funds for intersession, opportunities for parental involvement in the school, the provision of busses to attend educational events that may occur in local communities, and attention to the equitable distribution of cultural activities across tracks.

After having experienced a new calendar, one teacher described its benefits in this way:

> If the modified calendar continues, it will help families access support systems easier (psychologists, medical, tutors, parent support groups)—this vision of a supportive school community accessing many community resources is my personal dream for children.

Her vision of a school that reaches into the community, enabling better partnerships is educationally powerful. If this is combined with educational programs that first, are not detrimental, and second, enhance the opportunities of students for better academic and nonacademic achievement, the innovation is to be applauded.

On the other hand, we suggest it is educationally irresponsible to accompany the implementation of YRS by extravagant promises of higher test scores and improved academic achievement (particularly in the first few years) or to promise immediate or dramatic savings in the operational budget of the district. It is, however, appropriate to implement a YRS recognizing that it may help a school to move toward its goals of higher test scores or fiscal savings.

Responsible educational change requires accountability to all stakeholders who have legitimate interests in relevant political, social, fiscal, and educational issues. However, educational reform requires more than just responsibility to the status quo. Careful attention must also be paid to a consideration of whether the status quo is acceptable or desirable and to a determination that all students are able to benefit equally from their educational experiences.

MakingYRS an Equitable Change

For educational change to be *equitable*, it often requires strong leadership with a vision for a possibly different way of thinking about and organizing schooling. Too frequently, traditional aspects of schooling disadvantage some students and unfairly enhance or perpetuate the advantages of others. In our view, a desirable educational change takes seriously the need for an educational vision that sometimes challenges the accepted modes of operation and asks difficult questions about whose interests are, or are not, being served by the proposed innovation.

A *politically equitable* approach to year-round schooling ensures that all groups in the school community have access to the decision-making processes. This suggests that it is not equitable to introduce policy that disadvantages those who are not particularly comfortable with, or knowledgeable of, the political process. For instance, if a district establishes a policy that once a school exceeds a particular capacity it must change to a multi-track schedule, the policy should be implemented fairly in all schools. Sometimes we have seen such a policy overridden in areas where parents were perceived to have both negative responses to YRS and political clout. If the policy is responsible, then it should be implemented both responsibly and equitably. It should provide ways for both the economically advantaged and disadvantaged, the well-educated and the less knowledgeable, the English speaker and the non-English speaking member of the community to understand and have input into the decisions that will affect the education of all children in the community.

We suggest that if year-round schooling is to be *socially equitable*, the varying needs of different groups must be considered. One area in which equity needs to be applied is the assignment of students, teachers, and programs to tracks in a multi-track schedule. If policy permits parental and teacher requests to outweigh considerations of access and balance among tracks, then some students will continue to be disadvantaged, receiving education in more or less segregated classes with some of the least popular (and presumably, less talented) teachers. This may also isolate them in programs that provide little opportunity to interact with their peers across other social and economic levels. Placing all ESL programs on one track is an example of this. Likewise, policy that accepts parental requests to keep certain neighborhoods or communities together, without comparing the demographics of those communities to the whole school population, may be inequitable. Parents who are the most articulate or who have the greatest degree of comfort communicating with the school may request and receive what they perceive to be the "best tracks," leaving disproportionate numbers of students whose parents do not make requests on the other "less desirable" tracks.

To ensure social equity in a change like year-round schooling, planners need to recognize that a school's patrons may have different capabilities for participation, but that capacities may be built to include the voices of those who are traditionally not heard in educational decision making. *Capacity building*, according to Hargreaves and Fullan (1998) and Darling-Hammond (1997), is one of the requisite characteristics for successful educational reform. Darling-Hammond describes capacity building as helping people to "undertake tasks they have never before been called upon to accomplish" by teaching them to "think critically, to invent, to produce, and to solve problems" (p.40). We use the term to identify processes that help people to begin to develop an equitable, responsible, and sustainable approach to educational excellence.

If year-round schooling is to be *fiscally equitable*, there may be measures included to reduce differences in the academic achievement of students from different social, class, economic, or cultural groups. These may include targeted remedial measures during intersession to improve the progress of those who are not performing well, programs for parents, and innovative opportunities for enrichment.

All of these aspects taken together will help to ensure a fair and equitable approach to the educational issues related to year-round schooling. The calendar change may indeed be more *educationally equitable* for all students when disparities caused by summer learning loss are reduced and specific assistance is offered to students who are considered most in need. More regular breaks, an increasingly connected and sustained school year, greater opportunities for remediation or language training, all combined with better opportunities for teachers to plan for, and interact about, the needs of specific groups of students may indeed be good reasons to consider a year-round calendar. Provided that a decision to introduce year-round schooling does not ghettoize certain groups of students in separate programs on specific tracks, there is evidence that YRS has the capability to enhance the educational performance of students.

There is little point in introducing a calendar change, even when equity has been considered, if there is a sense on the part of participants that it is just another item in a long series of superficial educational change initiatives or that if they wait long enough it will go away. This is why, in our estimation, *sustainability* is the third criterion that needs to be considered when planning is initiated.

MAKING YRS A SUSTAINABLE CHANGE

There is a long history of educational change initiatives that begin with considerable fanfare and support only to die shortly thereafter with little assessment of whether the change had been effective or of why the change may have failed. Educators sometimes talk about LYNT (last year's new thing) and TYNT (this year's new thing), suggesting that if teachers simply wait out a change initiative, it will disappear. Adding to the general skepticism about the effectiveness of educational change is the perception that changes often occur in cycles. Cuban (1990) wrote an article entitled, *"Reforming, Again, Again, and Again,"* in which he likened educational change movements to the rhythm of a swinging pendulum, constantly moving between extremes. In the light of these common perceptions, we think the introduction of any educational change needs to consider the issue of sustainability.

We have discussed how the winds of political change can affect the *social sustainability* of an educational reform initiative, such as YRS, and how it may become captive to various campaign promises and the whims of an electorate. Where a calendar change is introduced as a short-term solution to a specific problem, such as overcrowding, it is generally seen as a transitory fix and not one that needs careful consideration of the issues of responsibility or equity. In some instances, where MT-YRS has been introduced merely as a temporary solution to a space issue, it has been accompanied by considerable resistance on the part of participants. This may be because, where there is little accountability for either the human or academic impact, there are few attendant positive effects of a calendar change. As is often the case with the erection of portable classrooms, so-called temporary fixes often become permanent institutions and need to be implemented with due care. Such temporary approaches may actually span the entire educational experience of some children. Because of this, it is important to ensure that even so-called temporary solutions are implemented with justice, equity, and integrity.

For a sustainable change to have the potential to positively affect both the culture and the structures of the implementing school or system, there needs to be a plan for sustainability built in from the outset. One aspect that must be carefully considered is the need for ongoing support and commitment on the part of the educational leaders as well as all participants. We have seen how in some districts the position of a designated contact person was eliminated shortly after the implementation of a YR calendar, leaving the principals of participating schools to fend for themselves when difficulties arose. In other districts, despite extensive public consultation during the initial implementation of a long-term plan, lack of ongoing communication helped to increase public misunderstanding and erode support.

Another aspect of sustainability is adaptability to the social and cultural needs of the constituents. Although we have suggested that sustainability is a requisite characteristic for successful implementation, it is not synonymous with inflexibility. A sustainable change is able to adapt to changing needs. We have seen that some schools that have begun as multi-track YR schools have changed to a single-track schedule and back again to a MT calendar, depending on fluctuating population patterns within their district. We have learned that some districts opened new schools on a single-track schedule to attend to the social needs for communication and community building within the school before moving to a multi-track schedule in a subsequent year.

Those implementing a *politically sustainable* restructuring initiative will need to consider the mobility and transience of North Americans as well as the fickleness of public opinion. It is not sufficient to establish a year-round calendar and to expect newcomers to a school or district to automatically understand and accept it. The failure to attend to ongoing communication sometimes results in the unfortunate situation of people moving into a district and showing up on the day after Labor Day to register their children for school, only to find they have missed the first four weeks of the term. In one area where this problem had become severe because of transfers in and out of a regional military base, the district showed adaptability by deciding that even its year-round schools would not begin the academic year prior to Labor Day. In other areas, the general volatility of the political climate may make the introduction of an innovation such as YRS especially complex.

Fiscal sustainability is a given for the ongoing success of any educational change. Although the institution of a year-round calendar may not, in and of itself, bring additional costs, and may, depending on the schedule adopted, actually save considerable amounts of money, there may well be attendant expenses required to ensure the sound and equitable educational programs discussed earlier. We saw, in one district, how a single-track schedule was introduced with great emphasis on the potential of its intersession programs to provide remedial and enrichment support for students. However, subsequent reductions in funds allocated for intersession resulted in the elimination of this part of the program. In other districts, no additional funds were provided to compensate administrators for the additional days of service. In still others, year-round principals were also expected to serve as unpaid principals of intersession, whereas their traditional-calendar counterparts received additional compensation for administering summer school programs. These are examples of the kinds of decisions that result in discontent and pressure to discontinue YRS. On the other hand, the change has a better chance of long-term success if a district recognizes that YRS may not necessarily reduce day-to-day operating expenses, but that the YR calendar has potential to improve its educational programs.

Educationally sustainable year-round programs, both single-track and multi-track, seem attractive because teachers and students find their stress and burnout are reduced and motivation and enthusiasm for learning increase. Teachers described having more opportunities to plan, organize and reorganize their approaches to instruction, and more time to reflect on their practice.

Many teachers reported that being on a year-round schedule facilitated their participation in such professional development activities as district wide in-service or university courses. These oppor-

tunities cannot be accidental. In a sustainable educational innovation, they must be planned. A district needs to ensure that if it offers in-service for a new program, it is available to all teachers regardless of schedule. This may require some additional funding to
encourage off-track teachers to participate during the year or to
provide substitute teachers to facilitate the attendance of teachers
in year-round schools for in-service scheduled during the traditional summer vacation.

A sustainable program will not result in the burnout of participants. We have previously raised the issue of administrator burnout and suggested that districts need to take proactive measures to
guard against it. Likewise, teachers who are permitted to teach
during every intersession may also eventually experience burnout.
In some instances, districts have asked specialist teachers to teach
on a full-year contract on a rainbow schedule without providing
additional modifications such as reduced, four-day work weeks, or
flexible vacation periods. In these cases, they have found, after just
a few years, that the schedule was too difficult for teachers to sustain. Sustainability of YRS in educational terms needs to provide
opportunities for the renewal and professional development of
participants as well as for the continuation of the programmatic
innovations that accompanied the year-round calendar from the
outset.

Considering the Matrix

We have suggested that thinking about each section of the matrix
presented in Figure 11.1 may be helpful in a consideration of the
appropriateness of a year-round school calendar. Our matrix is one
way to consider ideas related to educational excellence. It is not
intended to be an exhaustive treatment of the concepts of year-
round schooling.

Reflecting on whether a particular initiative is responsible, equitable, and sustainable requires careful examination of a large number of political, social, fiscal, and educational issues. It requires that
participants ask some difficult questions about who should be represented in the decision-making process, who will benefit from
particular modes of implementation, and whose interests may bet-

ter be served in different ways. It requires a long-term vision for educational excellence as well as effective leadership for change. Some of the relevant questions have been posed here. Others will be raised in the next few pages.

ADDITIONAL FACTORS AFFECTING SCHOOL REFORM

It is critical to recognize that consideration of the matrix, like any other discussion of a model for school reform, is incomplete without taking into account the unique questions that arise from specific contexts. Again, we stress that year-round schooling works best when it is carefully tailored to fit the local situation. Some relevant factors include policies on assessment and evaluation, perspectives on change processes, and the potential for innovative leadership.

Assessment and Evaluation

We have presented the matrix to serve as a reminder of some of the key areas for reflection, discussion, and debate about YRS. Elsewhere, we have referred to the inappropriateness of assessment or evaluation of year-round schooling (or any other educational change) during the early stages of its implementation. We do not want to leave the impression that assessment should not occur. On the contrary, assessment of an educational innovation, in both informal and formal ways, is essential and needs to be planned from the outset.

We emphasize that during the first year, ongoing feedback and correction, informed by interim or formative evaluation are necessary. These informal assessments should be used for internal consideration and course corrections and not produced for public dissemination or consumption. In general, summative, formal, or final assessments that occur prior to the third year of implementation could be harmful because they may cause inaccurate judgments about the impact of any innovation. Even though the information may be helpful, care should be taken that decisions about continuation or discontinuation of YRS not be based on premature evaluation.

Paradoxically, while we are urging that no formal assessment be conducted in the early stages of the implementation of YRS, we are also advocating that assessment, development of clear criteria, and the collection of baseline data begin prior to the actual implementation stage. For example, without baseline data concerning teacher absenteeism or incidents of student vandalism it is impossible to determine whether the introduction of YRS has had any impact on these areas. We have noted that, when many educational changes are introduced, they are formally assessed too early and then discarded before anyone has an opportunity to accurately appraise their potential to address the concerns for which they were originally instituted.

Underlying the evaluation of year-round schooling, or any other educational change, should be the bedrock principle that at a minimum, it not be detrimental to students. Once this has been established, it is important that the chosen assessment criteria relate directly to the original aims of the innovation. For instance, if multi-track year-round schooling is implemented to place additional students in buildings and save capital cost outlays, then this should be the primary focus of the evaluation. If the original goal in instituting a single-track model of year-round schooling is to increase flexibility of course offerings for students and improve student performance, then it should be assessed in that light. However, in a single-track model, the operating costs may rise to support programs that enhance student achievement. For that reason, the range of increased expenditures that a district is willing to sustain also needs to be predetermined. In other words, it is important to determine the parameters within which other effects, such as increased costs, are permitted to occur to meet the primary goal, such as increased student learning.

Reasonable methods of assessment are comprehensive. Appropriate fiscal assessment will calculate operating costs and short- and long-term capital outlays. Appropriate educational assessment will combine quantitative and qualitative measures to identify the impact of the reform on student achievement, attitudes, and behaviors, as well as on the overall culture and learning experiences within the school. Although they may show useful trends over time, standardized achievement tests should not be the sole indicators of student learning.

Appropriate assessment of a reform initiative needs to include, at minimum, all aspects of the matrix previously discussed. It is not adequate to consider the effectiveness of the reform apart from issues of equity and excellence for all students. Thus, when test scores are used as one measure of the reform's effectiveness, the data should be disaggregated to determine whether any groups of students are disadvantaged (or particularly advantaged) by the reform. If the impact of the calendar change on childcare is the particular focus of the evaluation, the responses of parents from lower income or single-parent families ought to be considered as well as those from two-parent, middle-class families.

The school cannot be easily separated from the community within which it is situated. Hence, the interests and welfare of all members of the community should be taken into account during an evaluation of the change. The calendar change itself may be incorrectly deemed to be effective or ineffective, appropriate or inappropriate, if it is judged in isolation from its context. Without an examination of the social, cultural, and political pressures related to the adoption, implementation, and continuation of the YRS initiative, it is difficult to determine whether challenges are related to the innovation itself or to outside factors that have affected the change. For example, where funding for intersession is withdrawn despite an explicit goal of improving the performance of at-risk students, YRS may be judged a failure when it is really the political decision about funding that is at fault.

Although a change of school calendar is a structural change, the assessment of its impact should take into consideration social, cultural, political, and fiscal factors as well as its impact on all groups having legitimate interests or stakes in the change itself. It should be assessed in terms of criteria identified at the outset, while taking into account appropriate timelines and baseline data. It should also permit the identification of unanticipated consequences that may be either positive or negative.

While each of these aspects of an evaluation is important, the educational impact of YRS should be the primary consideration in any assessment process. Even a finding of "no difference" in student achievement may be a satisfactory assessment, if other goals (such as fiscal savings or increased parental involvement) are achieved. However, in our estimation, the full benefits of YRS will not be realized unless its potential to positively affect student learning is exploited.

Change Processes

Much of the literature on educational change divides initiatives into categories: reform or restructuring, first-order or second-order change, reculturing or restructuring. In each case, there are theorists and practitioners who claim that one is a more useful, comprehensive, efficient, or effective way of considering change than the other.

In this book we have used the terms *reform* and *restructuring* quite loosely. Some experts like Darling-Hammond (1997) use *reform* to refer to a change that focuses on efficiency and controls; they reserve *restructuring* for a change that addresses the fundamental design of teaching and learning in schools. In our experience, the introduction of year-round schooling generally involves elements of both. It may well be implemented as an efficiency measure; indeed, it is referred to in some jurisdictions as one of many "efficiency schedules." But it may (and in our opinion, should) also act as a catalyst for more responsive and responsible education.

In his 1992 examination of some characteristics of educational restructuring initiatives, Murphy identified four major directions: organization and governance with specific emphasis on school-based management, voice and choice, teacher empowerment and professionalism, and teaching for meaningful understanding (p. 98). He indicated that recent restructuring initiatives highlighted a changed governance structure for education—one in which the focus moves from the school as the central unit of change to a recognition that the school needs to be considered as an integral part of a wider system or educational community (p. 102). It is clear that this discussion is applicable to an examination of year-round schooling because although the calendar change occurs at a school level, its successful implementation involves both district and community support and participation.

Murphy related his category of voice and choice to a "realignment of power and influence between professional educators and lay members of the community." He stated that the "traditional dominant relationship—with professional educators on the playing field and parents on the sidelines acting as cheerleaders or agitators or more likely passively watching the action—is replaced by a more equal distribution of influence" (p. 103). We have identified the important roles that parents, teachers, and administrators play in a change to year-round schooling. We have also argued that the change is unlikely to be sustained if traditional power relationships are maintained. However, where the base of support is widened and the community is seen as a partner in the educational endeavor, the likelihood of success is increased.

Teacher empowerment, in part, emphasizes the need to view teachers as professionals rather than as technicians. We have explored how increased time for renewal, reflection, organization, adaptation of practice, and a more professional, less stressful work schedule are reported by teachers to be benefits of a YRS calendar. It is our contention that these are related to teacher empowerment and professionalism in ways that have the potential to help teachers overcome the perception that they are simply technicians.

The theory that YRS tends to act as a catalyst for additional changes that may benefit the instructional programs of a school fulfills Murphy's (1992) last category. Successful restructuring involves a change that affects the teaching and learning core of a school. Students on a YR schedule perform at least as well on standardized tests and formal measures of educational achievement as their peers in traditional-calendar schools. There is the potential for at-risk students, in particular, to demonstrate less summer learning loss. Where intersession has been instituted, students benefit from new opportunities for remediation, acceleration, and enrichment. These considerations lead us to think that YRS is a strong and viable option for both educational reform and restructuring.

YRS is a change that may result in more efficient use of fiscal, human, and physical resources related to education. This type of change is sometimes referred to as structural or *first-order change*. YRS is a restructuring initiative with the potential to affect the very core of how we conceptualize teaching and learning. This is frequently termed *second-order change*. In our examination of year-round schooling, the distinctions blur. Most often, the relationships between new organizational structures and the central functions of teaching and learning are almost inseparable. From what we have learned about YRS, the distinction made in the last decade by change theorists that *reculturing* needs to come before *restructuring* appears to be somewhat fallacious. For example, Hargreaves and Fullan (1998) claim that restructuring is "part of the picture of successful reform" (p.119) but that it only works after "people have invested emotionally in transforming the culture and relationships in a school over many years" (p. 119). They support this contention by asserting that restructuring, which refers to "changes in the formal structure of schooling in terms of organization, timetables, roles and the like" has a "terrible track record" (p. 118). Reculturing, they maintain, changes the norms, values, and relationships within a school and encourages people to work differently.

We believe this position to be inaccurate. It does not appear to us that fundamental changes in school culture have had to occur over many years for a new year-round calendar to have a positive impact on teaching and learning. Indeed, in many instances, following a change in the *structure* of the school calendar, changes in the *culture* and relationships in the school and beyond its walls have occurred relatively quickly. Which comes first, restructuring or reculturing, appears akin to the chicken or the egg question. The answer to which comes first really does not matter. If year-round schooling is implemented intelligently, one seems to generate the other. The implementation of a year-round school calendar, when made carefully and appropriately, attending to the questions of responsibility, equity, and sustainability, seems to promote additional modifications in both culture and structure, changes that often reach the heart of the school: the quality of the teaching and learning.

Although the YRS calendar is neither inherently good nor bad, effective nor ineffective, close examination of many related aspects discussed in this book suggests that, when introduced with leadership and vision, YRS has the potential to be a highly beneficial innovation.

Innovative Leadership

It is not our intention here to engage in a theoretical discussion of leadership because that debate is as long as written history and just as inconclusive. It is, however, important to make explicit some of the assumptions that we have been working with as we have explored the viability of the concept of YRS and issues related to its implementation. We have not considered leadership to be either static or the sole attribute of any one individual, whether in a position of formal authority such as a school principal or district superintendent or not.

For this discussion, we accept the simple definition of leadership as "a process of influencing the activities of an individual or a group toward goal achievement in a given situation" (Hersey & Blanchard, 1977, p. 84). However, we recognize that no single individual either determines the goal or affects an organization's progress toward it. Although the definition does not make the notion of shared leadership or influence explicit, we believe these are integral to the fluid way leadership is exercised in successful YRS.

We also agree with Giddens' (1982) argument that no matter how great the imbalance of power, no one is entirely powerless. Many people within a school community "are very adept at converting whatever resources they possess into some degree of control" (p. 32). In this book, we have reported several instances in which people who seemed to have no formal power had tremendous influence over decision making related to YRS. Thus some form of leadership, no matter how informal, is shared among participants in any organization.

The leadership we have come to identify as useful for the examination and implementation of an educational change like YRS is fluid. It recognizes the importance of formal authority in that there is a need for those in designated leadership positions to influence policy to ensure that the reform is equitable and responsible. It takes into account the power of those not generally perceived to be powerful, offers them information they may not always have, and includes them in discussions about the central issues involved in the change. It acts responsibly.

We have seen that often district officials carefully select the people they believe will be the best and strongest principals for year-round schools. In turn, this may attract teachers who are both challenged by the quality of leadership they perceive to be present and intrigued by the opportunity to work within a newly structured calendar. This combination of a strong principal and teachers who have chosen the particular school may account for some of the success of year-round schools.

Foster (1986) asserted that *"leadership involves being politically critical and critically educative"* (p. 19, italics in original). By *politically critical*, he suggests that leaders need to recognize "alternative models" as well as the inequities and difficulties associated with current conceptions of reality. Leadership for YRS may come from anyone in the system, whether teacher, parent, principal, or administrator, who recognizes that there may be a different, perhaps even better, way to organize schooling for a given population.

Leadership that is *critically educative* involves both reflection on and analysis of practice. Critical leaders recognize that there are inequities in the present approach to schooling that need to be changed. They understand that power is not inherently negative, that it is necessary to exercise power to achieve the desired and agreed-on purposes. In this case, the purpose is the best possible education in responsible, equitable, and sustainable ways. To promote change, critical and educative leaders carefully analyze practice to identify problems and opportunities. They emphasize the merger of theory and moral practice that involves a search for ways of transforming practice to ensure it is just and equitable. Moral leadership implies a reflective approach to theory-in-use.

Leadership for educational change, that is both critical and educative, occurs simultaneously at different places in an organization. It challenges the present paradigm for educating children and seeks more equitable and more effective ways to organize schooling. In the case of YRS, it is most helpful if the concept is picked up by many people—educators, the general public, legislators, and policy makers. It is important for there to be formal support in the form of policy and resources as well as informal support in terms of enthusiasm and commitment.

YRS: A VIABLE EDUCATIONAL REFORM?

Kuhn (1970) wrote, "To be accepted as a paradigm, a theory must seem better than its competitors, but it need not, and in fact, never does, explain all the facts with which it can be confronted" (p. 18). Although Kuhn is talking about scientists, his description seems equally valid for educators. He states that there are always some who "cling to one or another of the older views" (p. 19) but that the reception of a new paradigm may sometimes be transformative.

We do not suggest that year-round schooling is a perfect educational solution. Neither have we advocated a wholesale change to a year-round calendar. In fact, we have asserted that the appropriateness of YRS for any given context needs to be determined by those within the situation and by those who will be most directly affected by its implementation. Nevertheless, we have shown that there are numerous myths related to year-round schooling that need to be dispelled. Many of the concerns are political rather than educational. Many difficulties are due to inequitable and irresponsible implementation rather than to the calendar itself. Much of the literature is ill founded and many reports of experiences with YRS are incomplete.

We have tried to present a thoughtful and careful examination of year-round schooling, its advantages and disadvantages, its problems and potential, as well as its theory and practice. When all of the factors are considered together, YRS can be a responsible, equitable, and sustainable educational innovation for the next century.

OUR FINAL WORD (FOR NOW)

We want to end on a more personal note. We doubt if it will be a surprise, even to the most casual readers of this book, but we are cautious supporters of YRS. When we started our research on YRS, our experience was limited to only one model and one form of district support. And we were not sure how well YRS worked. As our research progressed, we were amazed at the wide variety of YRS calendars and approaches to their implementation. We were surprised at the shortsightedness of some schools and districts, at their failure to look beyond the quick fix, at the missed opportunities, and at the limitations of their vision. We were also fascinated by the many wondrous ways year-round schooling had been enacted, at the flexibility and creativity of some schools, at the level of commitment evident in some districts, and at the range of opportunities provided for students. We came to understand that, when YRS was properly implemented and not just considered to be a stopgap measure until the next election, or the next change of superintendent, or until the district came into a windfall, it worked. The desire to tell the story of year-round schooling prompted us to write this book.

On the basis of our reading and research, we developed some strong opinions. The evidence appears solid that multi-tracking is not damaging or detrimental to students; in some cases, it may even offer academic benefits. It offers the greatest challenges and is the most difficult to implement—yet it offers the greatest opportunities for financial savings of any educational innovation we have seen in years. It is definitely better than the often used alternative of underpaid teachers and overcrowded classrooms—what we call "stack 'em deep and teach 'em cheap." It is also more fiscally accountable than building huge new public schools that lie empty several months of the year and many hours of each day.

When we think of single-track, we often wonder why it is not the calendar of choice for more districts. It holds much potential for improving the educational experiences of elementary and secondary school students as well as the work life of teachers. It opens doors to assist students in need of remediation or enrichment, those who need a more flexible schedule, who tend to burn out during the traditional school year, or who experience the most summer learning loss. It addresses concerns about the summer vacation period being too long, the school year being too short, buildings lying empty, and the agrarian calendar being outmoded. It offers a way to restructure and reculture that seems responsive to local community needs and supports the current emphasis on lifelong learning. And it contains the seeds of additional innovations such as intersession, new forms of team teaching, new ways of offering secondary school credits, and innovative community-based opportunities for learning.

So why do we say we are only "cautious" supporters of YRS? The advantages of year-round schooling may also be its greatest pitfalls. Single-track's advantage is that it opens the calendar to enhance opportunities for flexible and innovative learning. But sometimes, when it is implemented without reconsideration of instruction and without intersession, it seems to be simply change for the sake of change. In these instances, it may remain a superficial calendar modification without having any effect on the learning environment of students.

Multi-track's greatest advantage is its efficient use of space and its potential to save a district substantial amounts of money in capital outlay. But, often school district officials or policy makers get so caught up in trying to save educational monies, they forget to sweeten the pot a little. The pot that might feed the reform for YR education by enriching the diets of students and teachers cannot be left empty just to show how much money can be saved.

Thus, the pitfalls of both ST and MT-YRS relate primarily to what we call *fiscal shortsightedness*. We do not believe that too much money is currently being invested in education. And we are deathly afraid that where YRS results in substantial cost savings, the savings will be diverted from education rather than being reinvested for the good of the students.

We are cautious, therefore, because YRS can be used to save money at the expense of student learning. If YRS is implemented improperly, it can be at great cost to administrator, teacher, and student welfare. When consultation is foregone and involvement is discouraged, it may be harmful to the community and its relationship to the school.

YRS does best when programs are invented and innovations are nourished, when teachers are rewarded and students are cherished. Sometimes this means straying from the bottom line and putting back into the schools some of the money that has been saved by constructing fewer buildings. Always this means districts and states and provinces acting in the same generous spirit they expect from educators. Most of all, YRS does best when the education of children is put first.

APPENDIX A

OVERVIEW OF SOME COMMON YRS PLANS

The following three adaptations of a single-track calendar are usually introduced to provide additional educational opportunities for students.

Single-track: The whole school adopts a calendar in which some of the summer vacation time is redistributed as regular breaks throughout the school year. Sometimes, a 45-15 or 60-20 calendar is adopted, with intersession occurring during the breaks.

Dual-track: Some of the classes and teachers remain on the traditional school year calendar, whereas other classes and teachers in the same school adopt a modified school year, such as the 45-15. This offers flexibility of scheduling and accommodates a variety of preferences.

Secondary-school ST Quarter System: Some secondary schools use a ST quarter system to facilitate more flexibility in course completion. Students may attend an additional quarter in one of two ways, depending on the structure chosen. Sometimes an extra quarter is offered during the summer with voluntary attendance. Sometimes optional classes for credit are offered during intersession breaks between quarters.

Multi-track Schedules are often introduced to increase the number of students that may be accommodated in a given building. The following are some of the most common plans.

FOUR-TRACK SCHEDULES

45-15: This is one of the most common four-track schedules. Students attend school for 45 days (or nine weeks), followed by 15 days (or three weeks) of vacation. Each group of students is assigned to a track that rotates in an overlapping configuration so that at any given time, three fourths of the students are in school, and one fourth on vacation, thus providing a potential for 33% more students to be accommodated in the building.

60-20: This is the most common four-track schedule. Students are assigned to four tracks, each of which attends school for 60 days (or 12 weeks), followed by 20 days (four weeks) of vacation. As in the previous schedule, at any given time, three fourths of the students are in school, and one fourth on vacation, thus providing a potential for 33% more students to be accommodated in the building.

90-30: Basically the same as the previous schedules, except that students are in school for a longer period of time (90 days) with three vacation periods of 30 days each. This four-track schedule also increases a school's capacity by 33%.

FIVE-TRACK SCHEDULES

60-15: This calendar allows five groups of students to rotate on overlapping schedules of 60 days in school, followed by 15 days off. It permits a three-week common vacation for all students and staff while permitting a school to accommodate 25% more students than on the traditional calendar.

Quinmester: Another five-track calendar divides the year into five nine-week blocks with students attending four of the five terms (quins). It also permits an increased capacity of 25% but does not allow a common summer vacation.

OTHER SCHEDULES

Variations of the YR calendar are innumerable and include such combinations as the 15-5, 30-5, 45-10, 55-18, 60-10, or 65-20. Some more commonly implemented calendars include:

Concept Six: This is a three-track calendar divided into six terms of approximately 41 days each. On this schedule, students attend school fewer days than on a traditional calendar, but to compensate, each day is lengthened. Students are divided into three groups and, on a rotating basis, each group attends four terms. Only two tracks are in school at any one time. This permits an increase in school capacity of 50%.

Concept Eight: The curriculum is placed into eight 6-week blocks of time with students choosing six of the eight, thereby also having two 6-week vacation periods. This permits a 33% increase in capacity.

Orchard Plan: This is most commonly a variation of the five-track 60-15 schedule. Rather than rotate groups of students and their teachers, students within each class are divided into five groups or tracks. Only four tracks (or 80%) of the assigned students are in class at any one time. Thus, the teacher receives an extended-year contract (approximately 225 days), keeps his or her own classroom, and deals flexibly with students moving in and out of the classroom every 15 days. This also permits an increased capacity of 25%.

Other Flexible or Personalized Schedules: There are a number of flexible or individualized schedules suited to any alternative or magnet school in which students may often progress at their own pace. Permitting students to design their own schedules of 180 days in school offers variable increases in capacity.

APPENDIX B

ONGOING RESEARCH

For information about our ongoing, longitudinal, international research on year-round schooling, you may visit the authors' web pages at:

www.educationalresearch.com
www.edres.org

At our sites, you will find a listing of current publications about year-round schooling, links to other sites, as well as information about how to access additional resources.

GLOSSARY

Capital outlay—The amount of money a district spends on buildings and facilities, usually amortized over a term of 15, 20, or 25 years.

Critically low list—A list established by some state boards of education to identify schools in which the students are performing well below average on three or more measures of academic achievement.

Diversity—We use the term to refer to populations that are diverse in terms of class, parental level of education, ethnicity, and socioeconomic status as well as academic ability.

Effective—This term suggests that a school or district meets its defined educational goals for academic and nonacademic student outcomes.

Efficiency—This refers to a district that is accountable in terms of its fiscal expenditures and facility use. We do not imply that a business model is appropriate for the educational program, but that it is sometimes appropriate for resource allocation.

Efficiency schedule (or measure)—Any schedule that permits schools to maximize the number of students being accommodated in existing buildings.

Equity—By equity we mean a fair and just approach to all aspects of education, from programs and policy to expenditures and access to decision making. We do not suggest that equal is equitable, but that sometimes differential treatment is desirable to "level the playing field." Equity may demand a compromise between the democratic ideal of "one person, one vote" and ensuring that minority interests are protected.

Excellence—When we speak of educational excellence, we imply a program that offers the best possible educational experience for every student regardless of culture, race, gender, class, or SES.

Ghettoization—Involuntary grouping together of people that results in the creation of different classes of power, influence, prestige, or achievement, as when all ESL students are placed together on one track in a multi-track school.

Intersession—In a year-round school, this is the period of time between formally scheduled academic terms for given groups of students or teachers. Although no compulsory schooling occurs during intersession, individual schools may opt to introduce programs for remediation, enrichment, or acceleration that students may take on a voluntary basis.

Middle school—A term that applies to a school between elementary school and high school, generally for students between sixth and ninth grades. A middle-school philosophy attempts to achieve a more intimate and consistent grouping of students and teachers than in a high school. This is accomplished by organizing the curriculum so that students remain together for the core subjects, taught either by a single teacher, or a small team of teachers, who get to know each student well.

Nonacademic outcomes—The term refers to student attitudes, behaviors, dispositions, and achievements that are considered to be a legitimate part of what schools try to influence or teach, but that are not directly tied to specific subject matter and cannot be measured on standardized tests.

Off-track—In a year-round school, this refers to time not scheduled to be spent in-class. This is commonly referred to as school break or vacation time and may also be associated with intersession.

On-track—In a year-round school, this refers to the days scheduled for given groups (or tracks) of students and teachers to be in school. Individually, they may or may not correspond to an academic term, but taken together, represent the equivalent of a full school year.

Operating expenses—The annual costs of operating the educational programs in a school or district, including salaries, utilities, educational materials, and maintenance of buildings or grounds, but not the initial investment.

Rainbow track—The name given to the combination of rotating tracks, often known by names of colors, in a multi-track schedule. The term is sometimes applied to teachers whose assignments cut across several tracks.

Socioeconomic status (SES)—This term is a combination of the words *social, economic,* and *status* and recognizes that in our North American society, we often assign status according to these characteristics. Low socioeconomic status (SES) is associated with low levels of income, lack of formal education, and student "at-risk" characteristics, whereas high SES suggests that children come from advantaged homes with well-educated parents and higher than average income levels.

Track—This is the term used to designate the schedule of a group of students and teachers on a multi-track calendar, who rotate in and out of school together.

Track change—Going from a vacation period to in-school time or vice versa.

Traditional calendar—Also known as the agrarian calendar. This is the academic schedule that usually begins after Labor Day and ends early in the summer, with a break at Christmas, designated statutory holidays, and a long summer vacation.

REFERENCES

Alcorn, R. (1991). "Evaluation of Test Scores as a Measure of Success of Year-Round Schools in the San Diego Unified School District." San Diego, CA: San Diego Unified School District. Unpublished report.

Alcorn, R. (1993). "Year-Round School Information Packet." San Diego, CA: San Diego Unified School District. Unpublished report.

Alcorn, R. D. (1994). "Year-Round School Information Packet." San Diego, CA: San Diego Unified School District. Unpublished report.

Alkin, M. (1983). "Evaluation of the Year-Round Schools Program." Los Angeles Unified School District, CA. Research and Evaluation Branch.

Allinder, R. M., L. S. Fuchs, D. Fuchs, & C.L. Hamlett (1992). "Effects of Summer Break on Math and Spelling Performance as a Function of Grade Level." *The Elementary School Journal*, *92*(4), 451–460.

Atwood, N (1983). "Integration, Evaluation Reports: Appendix A Year-Round Schools Sub-studies, 1982–83." ED 246143.

Baker, G. (1990). "Parent Satisfaction with Year-Round and Traditional School Calendars in Conroe Independent School District." Unpublished master's thesis, Sam Houston State University, TX. ED 331137.

Baker, K., S. Pelavin, & R. Burnett (1978). "Comment on Effects of 'Extended School Year Operations.'" *Education*, *99*(2), 221–224.

Ballinger, C. (1987). "Unleashing the School Calendar." *Thrust for Educational Leadership*, *16*(1), 16–18.

Ballinger, C. (1988). "Rethinking the School Calendar." *Educational Leadership*, *45*(5), 57–61.

Ballinger, C., N. Kirschenbaum, & R. P. Poinbeauf (1987). "The Various Year Round Plans." The Year Round School: Where Learning Never Stops. Bloomington, IN: Phi Delta Kappa.

223

Banta, T. (1978). "Tradition Again Thwarts the Expanded School Year." *Phi Delta Kappan*, *59*(7), 491.

Barrett, T., R. T. Ferrett, & C. L. Beaty (1992). "Results of the Year-Round Education Parent, Staff, and Student Surveys." Riverside, CA: Department of Educational Accountability, RUSD. ED 358562.

Braddock, C., et al. (1997). "Report on Year-Round Education." Unpublished paper prepared by members of the University of Georgia/State University of West Georgia joint doctoral cohort program, November.

Bradford, J. C., Jr. (1993). "Making Year-Round Education (YRE) Work in Your District: A Nationally Recognized Single-Track Model." Prepared for the National School Boards Association National Convention, Anaheim, CA, March. ED 358559.

Bradford, J. C., Jr. (1996). "Year-Round Schools: A Twenty-Year Follow-up Study of a Nationally Recognized Single Track Four-Quarter Plan at the High School Level." Prepared for the American Educational Research Association, New York, April.

Brekke, N. (1983). "Cost Analysis of Year Round Education in the Oxnard School District." A paper presented to the 14th annual meeting of the National Council on Year-Round Education, Los Angeles, CA. ED 227597.

Brekke, N. (1985). "A Cost Analysis of Year Round Education in the Oxnard School District." A paper presented to the 16th annual meeting of the National Council on Year-Round Education, Los Angeles, CA. ED 260490.

Capps, L. R., & L. S. Cox (1991). "Improving the Learning of Mathematics in Our Schools." *Focus on Exceptional Children*, *23(9)*, 1–8.

Carpenter, S. (1977). "A Survey of the Attitudes of Parents of North Carolina Public Schools Toward Extended School Year Programs." PhD dissertation. Duke University.

Christie, S. (1989). "A Report on Opinion Surveys of Parents, Students, and Staff of Four-Track Year-Round Schools in Cajon Valley, 1987–1988." Cajon Valley, CA: Cajon Valley Union School District. ED 303888.

Cooper, H., B. Nye, K. Charlton, J. Lindsay, & S. Greathouse (1996). "The Effects of Summer Vacation on Achievement Test Scores: A Narrative and Meta-analytic Review." *Review of Educational Research*, *66*(3), 227–268.

Cordova, I., et al. (1970). "Evaluation of the Second Year (1968–69) of the Sustained Primary Program for Bilingual Students in Los Cruces, New Mexico." ED 052855.

Cuban, L. (1990). "Reforming, Again, Again, and Again." *Educational Researcher, 19*(1), 3–13.

Curry, J., W. Washington, & G. Zyskowski (1997) "Year-Round Schools Evaluation, 1996–1997." Austin TX: Austin Independent School District.

Darling-Hammond, L. (1997). "Reframing the School Reform Agenda: Developing Capacity for School Transformation." In E. Clinchy (Ed.), *Transforming Public Education*. New York: Teachers College Press.

Deason, D. (1975*)*. "A Study of Teacher Attitudes in Secondary 45–15 Year-Round School Programs." Ph.D. dissertation, U.S. International University.

Denton, J. J., & B. Walenta (1993). *"Cost Analysis of Year Round Schools: Variables and Algorithms."* College of Education, Texas A & M University. ED 358515.

Donato, R. (1996). "The Irony of Year-Round Schools: Mexican Migrant Resistance in a California Community During the Civil Rights Era." *Educational Administration Quarterly, 32*(2), 181–208.

Doyle, D. P., & C. E. Finn Jr. (1985). "Now Is the Time for Year-Round School." *Principal, 65*(1), 29–31.

Entwistle, D. R., & K. L. Alexander (1992). "Summer Set-Back: Race, Poverty, School Composition, and Mathematics Achievement in the First Two Years of School." *American Sociological Review, 57*, 72–84.

Entwistle, D. R., & K. L. Alexander (1994). "Winter Set-Back: The Racial Composition of Schools and Learning to Read." *American Sociological Review, 59*, 446–460.

Fass-Holmes, B., & K. Gates (1994). "Report on Single-Track Year Round Education in San Diego Unified School District, #689," San Diego City Schools.

Fine, M., L. Weis, & L. C. Powell (1997). "Communities of Difference: A Critical Look at Desegregated Spaces Created for and by Youth." *Harvard Educational Review, 67*(2), 247–284.

Foster, W. (1986). *The Reconstruction of Leadership*, Victoria: Deakin University Press.

French, D. A. (1992). "California Administrative Burnout and Year-Round Schools." A paper presented at the annual meeting of the National Association for Year-Round Education. ED 347660.

Fullan, M. G. (1991). *The New Meaning of Educational Change*, New York: Teachers College Press.

Fullan, M. (1993). *Change Forces*, New York: Falmer.

Furman, G. C. (1998). "Postmodernism and Community in Schools: Unraveling the Paradox." *Educational Administration Quarterly, 34,* 298–328.

Gandara, P. (1992). "Extended Year, Extended Contracts: Increasing Teacher Salary Options." *Urban Education, 27*(3), 229–247.

Gandara, P., & J. Fish (1994). "Year-Round Schooling as an Avenue to Major Structural Reform." *Educational Evaluation and Policy Analysis, 16*(1), 67–85.

Giddens, A. (1982). "Power, the Dialectic of Control and Class Structuration," in A. Giddens & G. Mackenzie (Eds.), *Social Class and Division of Labour: Essays in Honour of Ilya Neustadt.* Cambridge: Cambridge University Press.

Glines, D. (1988). "Year Round Education: A Philosophy." *Thrust for Educational Leadership, 16*(7), 14–17.

Glines, D. (1990). "Maximizing School Capacity." *Thrust for Educational Leadership, 19*(9), 49–53.

Goren, P., & R. Carriedo (1986). "Policy Analysis on the Implementation of an Expanded Multi-Track Year-Round School Program." San Diego, CA: Planning, Research and Evaluation Division, San Diego City Schools. ED 282328.

Greene, M. (1993). "The Passions of Pluralism: Multiculturalism and the Expanding Community." *Educational Researcher, 22*(1), 13–18.

Greenfield, T. A., (1994). "Year-Round Education: A Case for Change." *The Educational Forum, 58*(2), 252–262.

Greenwell, S., K. Ryan, B. Tinger, L. Motley, K. Barker, & L. Cheshure (1993). "An Evaluation Survey of Year-Round Education at North Layton Jr. High School." Unpublished document, Davis County Board of Education, Utah.

Grotjohn, D. K., & K. Banks (1993). "An Evaluation Synthesis: Year-Round Schools and Achievement." A paper presented to the annual meeting of the American Educational Research Association, New York, April.

Hargreaves A., & M. Fullan (1998). *What's Worth Fighting for Out There?* New York: Teachers College Press.

Harlan, M. (1973). "Academic Achievements of Students Enrolled in a 45–15 Continuous School Plan." PhD dissertation, Northern Illinois University.

Hazelton, J. E., C. Blakely, & J. Denton (1992). *Cost Effectiveness of Alternative Year-Round Schooling.* College of Business Administration, Texas A & M University. ED 354629.

Henderson, J. G., & R. D. Hawthorne (1995) *Transformative Curriculum Leadership.* Englewood Cliffs, NJ: Merrill/ Prentice Hall.

Hersey, P., & H. Blanchard (1977). *Management of Organizational Behavior: Utilizing Human Resources.* 3rd ed., Englewood Cliffs, NJ: Prentice-Hall.

Herman, J. L. (1991). "Novel Approaches to Relieve Overcrowding: The Effects of Concept 6 Year-Round Schools." *Urban Education,* 26(2), 195–213.

Heyns, B., (1987). "Schooling and Cognitive Development: Is There a Season for Learning?" *Child Development, 58,* 1151–1160.

Hill, B. (1980). "The Attitude of Patrons Toward Year-Round School in the Hillsboro, Oregon, Union High-School District," Ph.D. dissertation, Brigham Young University.

Hough, D., J.L. Zykowski, & J. Dick (1990). "Cost-Effects Analysis of Year-Round Education Programs." A paper presented at the annual meeting of AERA, Boston, MA. ED 319771.

Howell, V. T. (1988). "An Examination of Year-Round Education: Pros and Cons That Challenge Schooling in America." ED 298602.

Jamar, I. (1994). "Fall Testing: Are Some Students Differentially Disadvantaged?" Pittsburgh, PA: University of Pittsburgh, Learning and Development Center, June.

Kneese, C. C. (1996). "Review of Research on Student Learning in Year-Round Education." *Journal of Research and Development in Education,* 29(2), 61–72.

Kuhn, T. S. (1970). *The Structure of Scientific Revolutions,* Chicago: University of Chicago Press.

LaRocque, L. J., & C. M. Shields (1996). "Description and Analysis of School District Consultation Processes During Phase 1 of the British Columbia Year-Round School Study Project." Study conducted for the British Columbia Ministry of Education.

"Learning, Retention, and Forgetting." (1978). Technical report No. 5 for the Board of Regents of the State of New York, Albany, NY: New York State Department of Education and the University of the State of New York.

Levin, H. M. (1983). *Cost Effectiveness: A Primer.* Beverly Hills, CA: Sage.

Los Angeles Unified School District. (1983). "Integration Evaluation Reports: Executive Summaries and Evaluation Designs, 1982–83." Publication No. 437. Los Angeles, CA: Research and Evaluation Branch, LAUSD. ED 246144.

Los Angeles Unified School District. (1986). "Early School Leavers: High School Students Who Left School Before Graduating, 1982–1983." Publication No. 458. Los Angeles, CA: Research and Evaluation Branch, LAUSD. ED 312349.

Mark, M. M., & R. L. Shotland (1985). "Stakeholder-Based Evaluation and Value Judgments." *Evaluation Review, 19*(15), 605–626.

Matheson, R. (1993). "Toward Being an Informed Consumer: A Year-Round Education Mandate." *ATA Magazine. 73*(4), 34–37.

Matty, E. J., (1978). "The 45–15 Year-Round School: An Evaluation of First-Year Algebra Achievement of Selected Ninth Grade Students." Ph.D. dissertation, University of Arizona.

McDaniel, W. (1976). "A Study of the Attitudes of Selected Groups of Citizens in Onondaga County Toward the Year-Round School Concept." Ph.D. dissertation, Syracuse University.

McDaniel, P. (1993) "Making it Happen: How to Handle the Politics of Year-Round Education." *The Year-Rounder*, Fall, 4–9.

McNamara, J. R. (1981). "A Computer-Based Method for Student Assignment and Optimal Tract Balancing." *Association for Educational Data Systems Journal*, Winter, 57–72.

Merino, B. J. (1983). "The Impact of Year-Round Schooling—A Review." *Urban Education, 18*(3), 298–316.

Murphy, J. (1992). "School Effectiveness and School Restructuring: Contributions to Educational Improvement." *School effectiveness and school improvement, 3*(2), 90–109.

Mutchler, S. E. (1993). "Year-Round Education." *SEDL Insights,* 2–6, Austin, TX: Southwest Educational Development Lab. ED 363966.

National Education Association. (1987). *Year-Round Schools.* Washington, DC: NEA, "What research says about:" Series, #8, ED 310486.

National Education Commission on Time and Learning. (1994). *Prisoners of Time: Schools and Programs Making Time Work for Students and Teachers.* Washington, DC: Government Printing. ED 366115.

Noddings, N. (1992). *The Challenge to Care in Schools.* New York: Teachers College Press.

O'Neil, I. R., & D. R. Adamson (1993). "When Less Is More." *The American School Board Journal*, April, 39–41.

Peltier, G. L. (1991). "Year-Round Education: The Controversy and the Research Evidence." *The NASSP Bulletin,* September, 120–129.

Perry, L. (1991). "Should We Have a New School Clock and a New School Calendar?" *Education Canada, 31*(2), 8–15.

Quinlan, C., C. George, & T. Emmett (1987). "Year-Round Education: Year-Round Opportunities—A Study of Year-Round Education in California." California State Department of Education.

Rasberry, Q. (1994). "Year-Round Schools May Not Be the Answer." A paper presented at the Conference for Private Childcare Centers and Preschools, Orlando, FL. ED 369548.

Richmond, M. J. Jr. (1978). Richmond's response to comment by Keith Baker and others, *Education*, 99(2), 225–228.

Ricketts, A. R. (1976). "An Examination of Year-Round School in District 11." Ph.D. dissertation, University of Colorado.

Russell, C. (1976). "Split Shift and Year-Round Schools: Two Non-traditional Methods of Organizing School Time." Ph.D. dissertation. University of Arkansas.

Sardo-Brown, D., & M. Rooney (1992). "The Vote on All-Year Schools." *The American School Board Journal*, July, 25–30.

Senge, P. M. (1990). The Fifth Discipline: The Art and Practice of the Learning Organization. New York: Doubleday/Currency.

Sergiovanni, T. J. (1994). "Organizations or Communities? Changing the Metaphor Changes the Theory." *Educational Administration Quarterly*, 30(2), 214–226.

Serifs, D. (1990). "Year Round Education: A Closer Look." ED 329008.

Shields, C. M., & L. J. LaRocque (1997). "Reflections on Consultative Decision-Making: Challenging Concepts of Best Practice in a Provincial Change Initiative." *The Canadian Administrator*, 36(7), 1–9.

Shields, C. M., & S. L. Oberg (1995). *"What Can We Learn from the Data? A Preliminary Study of Schools with Different Calendars."* A paper presented at the annual meeting of the Canadian Society for Studies in Education, Montreal.

Shields, C. M., & S. L. Oberg (1997). "Exploring the Myths: A Comparison of Parents' Attitudes to Traditional and Multi-Track Year-Round School Calendars." *Journal of Educational Administration and Foundations*, 2(2), 42–60.

Shields, C. M., & S. L. Oberg (1999). "What Can We Learn from the Data? A Study of the Effects of Different School Calendars on Student Outcomes." *Urban Education*, 34(2), 125–154.

Shields, C. M., & P. A. Seltzer (1997). "Complexities and Paradoxes of Community: Towards a More Useful Conceptualization of Community." *Educational Administration Quarterly*, 33(4), 413–439.

Six, L. (1995). "A Review of Recent Studies Relating to the Achievement of Students Enrolled in Year-Round Education Programs." San Diego, CA: National Association for Year-Round Education.

Smith, D. B. (1992). "Finding Room for California's Children." *Thrust for Educational Leadership*, 21(6), 8–15.

Smith, W. J., et al (1998), Student Engagement in learning and School Life: *National Project Report*. Montreal, PQ: McGill University, Office of Research on Educational Policy.

Stiff, D. (1986). "Year-Round School: Some Constraints to Consider." *Thrust for Educational Leadership, 15*(October), 12–17.

Taylor. J. (1993). 21st Century School Calendar Task Force: Report. Corvallis, Oregon.

Virginia State Department of Education. (1992). *"Instructional Time and Student Learning: A Study of the School Calendar and Instructional Time."* U.S. Dept. of Education. ED 356555.

Warrick-Harris, E. (1995). "Year-Round School: Best Thing Since Sliced Bread." *Childhood education,* annual theme, 282–287.

Weaver, T. (1992). "Year-Round Education." ED 342107.

Webb, M. (1973). "A Comparative Analysis of Some of the Concerns and Attitudes of Secondary Classroom Teachers with Respect to the Year-Round Schools." Ph.D. Dissertation, Ohio University.

Webster, W. E., & K. L. Nyberg (1992). "Converting a High School to YRE." *Thrust for Educational Leadership, 21*(6), 22–25.

Weinert, R. (1987). "Designing Schools for Year Round Education." *Thrust for Educational Leadership, 16*(May/June), 18–19.

Weiss, J. (1993). "Changing Times, Changing Minds: The Consultation Process in Considering Year-Round Schooling." Toronto: OISE. ED 371469.

White, W. D. (1987). "Effects of the Year-Round Calendar on School Attendance." A paper presented at the annual meeting of the National Council on Year-Round Education, Anaheim, CA. ED 280157.

White, W. D. (1988). "Year-Round High Schools: Benefits to Students, Parents, and Teachers." *NASSP Bulletin,* January, 103–106.

White, W. D. (1992). "Year-Round No More." *American School Journal, July,* p.27–30.

Winters, W. L. (1995). "A Review of Recent Studies Relating to the Achievement of Students Enrolled in Year-Round Education Programs." San Diego, CA: National Association for Year-Round Education.

Worsnop, R. L. (1996). "Year-Round Schools: The Issues." *CQ Researcher, 6*(19), 435–443.

Young, R. J., & D. E. Berger (1983). "Evaluation of a Year-Round Junior High School Operation." *NASSP Bulletin,* January, 53–59.

Zykowski, J. L., D. E. Mitchell, D. Hough, & S. E. Gavin (1991). "A Review of Year-Round Education Research." Riverside, CA: California Education Research Cooperative. ED 330040.

INDEX

Please note that numbers in *italics* refer to figures.

teachers, year-round schooling and, 101–15; literature on, 102–3; and organizational issues, 107–12; and personal issues, 104–7
track assignments, year-round schooling and, administrator views of, 127, 129
track change, definition of, 221
tracks, 11; definition of, 221
traditional calendar, 2, 4–5; definition of, 221
transitional costs, 181–82
TYNT (this year's new thing), 200

vacation scheduling, parents on, 94–95
vandalism, year-round schooling and, 84
villages, 56–57

Virginia State Department of Education, 25

year-round schooling (YRS), 1–5, 191–214; adapting models of, 62–63, *64;* administrative issues in, 125–30; administrator views of, 119–32; community in, 144–49; conceptual matrix for examination of, 193–204, *194;* contexts of, in North America, 154–56; evaluation and assessment of, 168–69, 204–7; fiscal issues with, 174–89; models and practice of, 9–69; political considerations with, 152–73; at secondary level, 48–69; and students, 75–87; viability of, 211–12